META-TRENDS AND THE NEXT ECONOMY

BY MARK PARROTT

AND COLE PARROTT

MOtivational PRESS

LEADERS IN GLOBAL PUBLISHING

Published by Motivational Press, Inc.
1777 Aurora Road
Melbourne, Florida, 32935
www.MotivationalPress.com

Manufactured in the United States of America.

ISBN: 978-1-62865-454-7

CONTENTS

INTRODUCTION

In my travels as a professional speaker with Vistage, I speak to CEOs of the private middle markets. Vistage is the largest CEO organization in the world. At the time of this writing, it currently has 22,000 members. According to Ohio State University, these CEOs have between 10 million 1 billion in revenue, and are privately held. I am amazed at how good these CEOs are at managing the day-to-day operations of owning a business—they work an average of 55 hours a week chasing the American dream. I am equally amazed at how little time they spend looking into the future, in other words, they work in the business instead of on it. They tend to be so busy with the day-to-day, but they spend little, if any, time researching and planning the future. The truth is, most lack the knowledge or the ability to interpret the data predicting the health of their industry or knowing their client/customer, and if they did their companies would be more resilient, durable and sustainable.

"Know thyself," attributed to Aristotle

"Know thy customer," attributed to Mark Parrott

The challenges of knowing thy customer:

Where to find the information on the buying habits of people?

What age is the peak age of the customers that purchase my product or service?

How many people are entering that peak age, in other words, what are the trends?

I was presenting in Milwaukee to a large group and the topic of the true role of the CEO came up. A rather large teddy bear of a CEO said, "I know what that is." He then regaled us with a story of a new hire in the company who was at an employee barbecue. This recruit approached the CEO and asked the question, "So, what do you do?" The CEO looked inquisitively at him and said, "What do you mean, what do I do?"

Now, this can mean one of two things: either, the new hire was too stupid to know who the CEO is or, more likely, the CEO was not part of the hiring process (I prefer to believe the latter). After the CEO asked the man to explain his question, he then turned to the other employees, pointing out the head of sales and the head of distribution among others and returned to the original question, "So what do you do?" The CEO carefully measured the question this time and then stated, "I make sure you have a job in five years." With that, the new hire realized his faux pas, and, with his jaw agape, he blurted out, "Well, keep up the good work," and then ran away with his tail between his legs.

Although this is a funny anecdote, and it may be embarrassing to that new hire personally, I believe they were both right. The true role the CEO is to make sure that man has a job in five years. If you extrapolate to include all employees, the only *real* role of the CEO is to make sure **ALL** the employees have a job in five years—and he should keep up the good work. This work is noble and it's necessary.

WHAT LEADERS NEED TO PROVIDE: C. A. N. E. R.

It is my belief that all leaders need to provide what I've come to call

C. A. N. E. R., which stands for:

C. Constant

A. And

N. Never

E. Ending

R. Reassurance

The CEO/business leader must go to great lengths to provide this constant reassurance to those who follow him or her; they must do this for the betterment of themselves, their company and the economy, as a whole.

There is a big movement in leadership training toward authentic leadership, and sometimes that's misinterpreted, in my opinion, to mean blatantly honest. I am all for authenticity, but authentic to what? We want to be authentic to the role of CEO, meaning our direct reports/employees deserve for us to provide constant and never-ending reassurance; which means we need to answer their real questions. For example, when they ask us, "How's business going?", what they're really asking us is, "Do I have a job next year?" Business owners, especially relatively new ones, will make the mistake of using their employees as therapists or sounding boards for ideas, but it's not the employee's responsibility to keep this from happening, it's the CEO's. Authenticity plays out with this research you are about to read in that you need to do whatever it takes to provide that reassurance, whether it's more training, research, therapy—whatever it takes. A CEO's true role is to provide that reassurance. This book is all about planning the future, which is an essential ingredient in providing reassurance.

Steven Pinker, author of the best-selling book *How the Mind Works*, would tell you that the majority of people see the world through a lens of fear. I agree and would argue they also see the **FUTURE** through a lens of fear. It is my strong belief that the study of demographics leads one to know their customer better and therefore one can strategically plan and/or develop a marketing plan more accurately, thus going a long way toward providing the reassurance that's required of the business leader position.

"If you want to get rich, concentrate your assets. If you want to stay rich, diversify your assets." —accredited to an unknown economist (if I keep saying this I might as well attribute it to myself)

The overwhelming majority of business owners are under-diversified simply because they own a business. Ninety percent of their net worth is tied up into the business itself, and any advisor leaving Investing 101 can tell you that you should never have, on average, 90 percent of your net worth tied up in one investment. The paradox exists that unless you qualify as under-diversified, you can't own a business.

Two-thirds of the American economy is retail sales. And in retail sales, knowing your customer is of paramount importance. When you understand the peak age of your customer and how many people are turning that age, you go a long way toward assuring the success of your business and making safe the financial lives of those who count on you. This book can show the way, and **the way to utilize this book is as a diversification tool.**

How to employ this book as a diversification tool:

» Understand how spending affects the economy
» Understand how spending affects your portion of the economy

This book can be used to create wealth through concentrating assets in a business, or it can teach you how to stay wealthy through the diversification of your assets and/or customer base. By studying the statistics represented in this book, you'll know which industries will thrive in the next few decades. If you are currently running a business, you'll know how to diversify your business into products and services which will thrive in the next few decades. You will also know how to pivot, in other words, how to stay relevant in the economy in the next few decades, if you're not already one of the lucky few that's currently positioned appropriately.

If you're one of the lucky industries that will thrive in the next few decades, you'll know by reading this book which industries to diversify your windfalls into in order to stay wealthy.

If you're starting a business, you'll know which industries will thrive and which ones will make sense to start in the coming years.

College students will need to know which fields of study they should pursue in order to apply this knowledge. Reading this book will help them do so.

Investors, after reading this, you'll know which areas of the economy to invest in.

Either way, business leaders have potentially hundreds to thousands of lives (depending on the size of their business) counting on them to make excellent decisions each and every day. And the hours spent reading this material will go a long way toward helping them do so.

Unfortunately, demographics is only part of the economic story. This book is not designed as a market timing service, as some of my peers would have you believe. The economy is wrought with unknowable variables. The best way to view the data is more like the moon phases, which ultimately determine the tide. Knowing the peak spending age of each of the products or services is knowing when the tide of money is moving in for a product or service or moving out. Knowledge is power, and knowing which industries will thrive in the coming decades is ultimate power.

The US government is wonderful at collecting data. It collects the data in two major ways: by survey and census. The surveys are conducted by interview for major purchases like homes, cars, etc., or by a diary, meticulously maintained over two weeks in order to track items purchased that are likely to be easily forgotten.

Unfortunately, the US government does no forecasting with said data, so the goal of this book is not just to inform you of which industries will thrive but to increase your knowledge and enable you to become a forecaster of your chosen industry. Knowing the demographic spending patterns will enable you to be a better forecaster.

We're going to study more than 200 consumer products in this book, so the book will go a long way to satisfying your data needs. It is improbable, however, to say the book will be all of what you need. The data not collected by federal mandate can be obtained in other ways, and in future chapters, I will advise you on how to fill in the gaps.

The science of data collection and dissemination is profound—the art of interpreting that data is up to you. Happy hunting!

CHAPTER 1

DEMOGRAPHICS: WHAT ARE THEY? AND WHY ARE THEY SO IMPORTANT?

Any economist worth his salt will tell you economy breaks down into thirds. **One-third is the government**, meaning a government's power to manipulate interest rates, control the money supply, and spend. **Two-thirds is the population**, meaning the population's power to spend, also known as consumer spending. Anyone with a fourth-grade education can tell you that two-thirds is greater than one-third. The direct correlation between the population and the shape of the economy merely illustrates that the United States is addicted to its own consumer spending. And as the population goes, so shall its economy.

So, the US government has the power to:

MANIPULATE INTEREST RATES

The government has the power to manipulate interest rates on both the long and short end of the spectrum of interest rates. The short-term interest rate is referred to as the discount rate (which is the interest rate charged to commercial banks and other depository institutions for loans received from the Federal Reserve Bank). Most people think the Federal Reserve controls all interest rates; really what it does is influence them.

Long-term interest rate manipulation is typically done by the government buying and or selling long-term bonds. The government can act in an effective, powerful way as an acquirer of long-term bonds. With the ability to print money and buy bonds, the government has the ability to unlock scared bond markets, much as it did in unfreezing the long-term bond market during the financial crisis of 2008-2009.

CONTROL THE MONEY SUPPLY

This aspect of government power consists of buying and selling government securities by the Federal Reserve, such as treasury bills from large banks and securities dealers. For example, buying bonds increases money supply in the hands of the public. The bonds were bought in exchange for dollars. Once those dollars are in the hands of the banks (banks are typically the sellers of loans, which are technically bonds), the banks can then lend those dollars to future borrowers who spend that money on major purchases such cars, houses, business start-ups, etc., thus putting those dollars into circulation. Selling government securities takes money out of the hands of the banks and puts it back into the hands of the government, in effect taking it out of circulation.

Another means of controlling the money supply has to do with manipulating large banking institutions' capital reserve requirements. The net effect is to reduce and or increase the money that banks have on hand to lend.

The government's ability to spend and possibly affect the economy is usually affected by policy makers on whatever initiatives the government is looking to emphasize. For example, in the Great Depression of the 1930s, workforce programs such as the Civilian Conservation Corps (CCC) and the Works Progress Administration (WPA) were instituted as a means to putting people back to work. Recently in the financial crisis, the government made huge investments in infrastructure and green energy.

The ability to predict what the government will or will not do is ridiculously difficult and fraught with inaccuracy due to the power being in the hands of the few. Predicting what one person or a small group of people are likely to do is ridiculously difficult, and discussion of such is the domain of the popular press. I believe predicting what the government will do borders on the dramatic, the compelling, and the scary, all of which sell ad space in the popular press. The human mind is hardwired to pay attention to threats, so it seeks out the unpredictable and the scary as a survival tool. This plays into the hands of the media. This book focuses on what the population will do, not what the government is likely to do.

The good news for us is the population is ridiculously predictable and therefore a wonderful foundation for strategic planning. So whether you're an investor, a business owner, or a professional counselor (financial, legal, etc.), studying these predictable trends and knowing how many people will enter those magic age groups gives you clarity to predict.

The population's power to spend is where we need to focus our attention. It doesn't take a genius to do the simple math: if two-thirds of the economy is spending by the population, that is what we should focus our attention.

So the good news for you, the reader, is that studying the population's power to spend is not dramatic, compelling, or threatening—its boring! So boring it's predictable decades in advance. Therefore, it's wonderful material for you the reader to utilize when evaluating your future plans.

UNDERSTANDING POPULATION SPENDING TRENDS:

Helps us with strategic planning

Helps us with marketing planning

Helps us with financial planning

What the population does, although valueless to the media, is increasingly valuable for us. Having the power to predict decades in advance the spending patterns of the average person is of enormous financial benefit for those working in and or running companies. Most people think others see the world the way they do. Not true. This work will have you walk a mile in the shoes of the average person to help you identify the threats and the opportunities the future holds, all while identifying which industries will thrive in the next 15 years. *This will enable anyone to start the right business and/or implement a profitable plan to minimize threats while maximizing opportunities*—even which countries are likely to thrive, just as ours begins to falter—and in my opinion, it *will* falter. This is game-changer information in order to create a proper diversification strategy.

To begin our understanding of demographics and their economic benefit, we first need to identify the most economically beneficial age group. In my presentations across North America, I have CEOs and C-level executives play what I call the "age game." Their answers are telling. Before I show you their most common answers, let's play the game.

The game highlights three age categories, people in their 30s, 50s, 60s. I ask four questions while requesting a show of hands for how many people in the room think the answer to the question is one age group or another; for example, how many people think 30-year-olds spend the most money in the United States today?

Which age group spends the most money?

Which age group produces the most money for their business or corporation?

Which age group earns the most money?

Which age group invests the most money?

I think you would agree that each of these answers involves economically beneficial activities, and understanding which age group does each of them the most is a powerful way to identify economically beneficial age groups.

THE AGE GAME

	30	50	60
Spends the most			
Produces the most			
Earns the most			
Invests the most			

Without overthinking it, consider which one of these categories you would choose to answer each of the questions, and I'll show you what the majority answers are for each one of them.

I've conducted this exercise with over 8,000 CEOs of the private middle markets, with an additional 6,000 or so C-level executives. These results border on empirical research and corroborate a lot of the theories on employee productivity and spending/income peaks from the Bureau of Labor Statistics.

Results of the exercise:

The age game

30   50   60

The most common answer from CEOs the program in markets

Spends the most: is the 50-year-old age group

Produces the most: is the 50-year-old age group

Earns the most: is the 50-year-old age group

Invests the most is the 50-year-old age group

When I conduct this exercise, each category receives a certain amount hands in the air, with the exception of 30-year-olds investing the most, which receives none. Asking these four questions is like doing a live survey, and the answers are telling. More important than that is to understand the **first hypothesis** in understanding demographics and their effect on the economy:

THE EARLY 50S IS THE MOST BENEFICIAL AGE GROUP TO THE ECONOMY

People in their early 50s are the most economically beneficial age because they spend the most, earn the most, produce the most, and invest the most.

For the purposes of increasing the accuracy of economic predictions for the United States, we need to focus on "spends the most," because as our population spends, so does our economy grow. Ask yourself can you think of any economy in the world that is more addicted to its own consumer spending than the United States? The majority of my audiences says no, there is no economy in the world more addicted to its own consumer spending than our own. To emphasize this, all one needs to do is to realize that we have a massive trade deficit with the rest of the world. Due to this trade deficit, the US is a net importer of other countries' goods and services. The **second hypothesis** is that any economy will only be as healthy as however many peak-spending-age people it has in it.

One could even argue that you can tell the health of any economy in the world based on how many peak-spending-age people the country has. More important than understanding how many is understanding the trends. If the country has more peak spenders coming in the next decade, we can expect good times and an expanding market. Conversely, if the economy is decreasing in the number of peak spenders, we expect a tough decade, and maybe we'll need to tighten our belts. To that effect, we need to fully understand the population charts.

Prior to this theory, I thought the population was slowly increasing each year, and when I visualized the population, I saw it as a straight line increasing slightly as we went forward by an approximate 2.1% (illustrated by a healthy fertility/birth rate). I did not realize that populations undulate, nor could I have imagined how that undulation affects each of the areas of the economy, for example, the educators' market. The fact that municipalities needed to build schools in the 50s, 60s, and 70s and then closed them in the 80s was predictable decades in advance, but, as it turns out, that's not how governments react. They are rarely, if ever, proactive. Rarely do they fix tomorrow's problems today; usually they fix yesterday's problems today. The cynic might even say they create tomorrow's problems today. We will cover future political challenges brought on by the aging of the population in later chapters.

For now, we need to understand the effects that undulations in population have on our economy.

In a world that changes so rapidly, we have to take a step back and realize in our distant past that each generation's lives would seem very similar to the previous generations, whereas now there is an enormous difference between people born only decades apart. Understanding these differences and the trends is of vast value to companies and investors alike.

I differ from other demographers in that we see the breakdown of the generations into six categories, not seven, and the start year and end year of said generation is different from the categories used by the US Census. These differences measure more than just semantics. We see little value in following previous demographers like lemmings. In fact, the Bureau of Labor Statistics and the US Census just decided arbitrarily when to begin and end a generation. What is of utmost importance is understanding demographics from a peak-to-trough perspective, so we will be renaming the generations based on the years they start and eliminating one of the generational categories (which tends to create needless confusion while significantly increasing the predictability, and therefore the value, of this information.

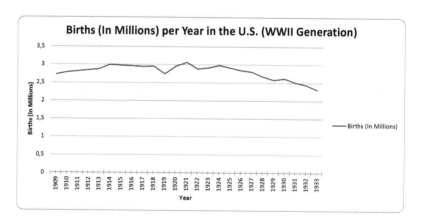

The WWII generation born pre-1933

Once a major force in American culture, this is our oldest living generation; it helped propel America to become the economic juggernaut and leader of the free world. This generation saw the first flight, the largest war, and the moon landing, and, partly as a result of winning the World War II, had a ridiculous number of children now known as the baby boom generation.

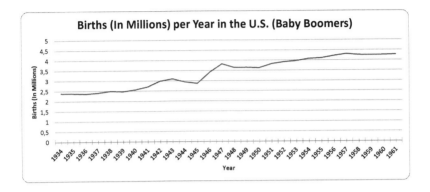

Baby boom generation, *born 1933 through 1961*

This is a deviation from the Census' version of the baby boom generation (typically 1946 to 1964), which includes a category known as the "swing generation." It is my belief is that this is just the first wave of the baby boom generation, born prior to World War II. The census breaks down the next two waves born post-World War II and during the 60s. This eliminates some confusion, for example, that some experts think the millennial generation is larger than the baby boom generation, giving false hopes to certain categories of industries that would thrive as a result if that were true.

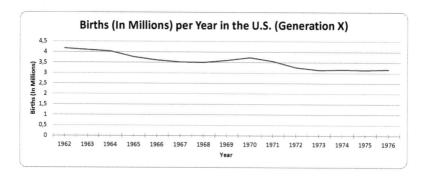

Generation X, *born 1962 through 1976*

This category was previously known as the baby bust generation due to its decreasing number of births, ultimately bottoming out in 1976. I myself am an early generation Xer and felt like I was living in the shadow of the baby boom—whether it was advertisers or media types ignoring our needs or was simply more profitable to pay attention to the baby boomer generation. This left gen-Xers feeling like the forgotten generation.

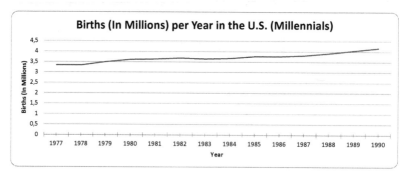

Millennials, *born 1976 through 1990*

Some fantastic contextual differences between these generations shows up dramatically in the millennial generation, according to Julie Lythcott-Haims, author of *How to Raise an Adult* and former dean of Stanford University, on children born after "America's Most Wanted" became the number-one television show in the United States, changing parenting for this generation. Parenting went from coaching the child from a distance to becoming the taxi driver and program director. The good news is that millennials were not abducted and/or molested in great numbers. The downside of all this parental attention however, is that many millennials are entirely reliant on others for direction. This presents both challenges and opportunities for employers.

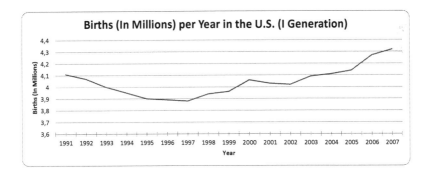

Births (In Millions) per Year in the U.S. (I Generation)

The I generation, *born 1990 through 2007*

This population is sometimes referred to as the "digitally native" generation, meaning they grew up in the era of computers and the Internet, and some might say they are tethered to this technology. This generation's identity is still currently forming, and it will be fascinating in the coming decades to see what they become. As the parent of four boys from this generation, I myself am particularly attentive to it.

The recession generation, *born post 2007*

The effects of economic strife brought on by the great recession significantly delayed childbirths, decreasing annual live childbirths to a recent low. According to the Center for Disease Control (CDC), the birth rate in the US has dropped by more than 2% since 2000, and 1.5% of the 2% was after 2008. Because this generation is still forming, I cannot say that there is a high degree of accuracy when predicting what they will or will not do, nor is it statistically significant enough to warrant examination.

In the next chapter, I will walk you through the life event timeline so you can fully understand just how predictable the average person really is.

CHAPTER 2

MEET THE MODERN-DAY MAN/ WOMAN

This chapter introduces the reader to the gasoline that fuels the economy. Looking behind the mask of our economic juggernaut reveals the secret sauce for industrialized economies.

Chances are you, the reader, don't represent the average person or woman simply because you are actually reading this book. To let you in on a dirty secret: According to best-selling life coach and author Tony Robbins (in a presentation I attended), self-improvement books, especially in the financial world (and the overwhelming majority of bestsellers), although bought or sometimes received as gifts, are never even read. Something like only 10 percent that are bought are actually read. So if you're reading this now, you're better than 90 percent of the people who even purchase this type of book, which makes you rare.

Also rare are my audiences in New York and California, where I have to get them to dispel their statistical disbelief around national statistics about young people moving out of their parents' homes. Real estate prices in these two markets are so prohibitively expensive that people do not start their "life event timeline" as young as those who grow up in middle America. So the exercise I run in my presentations asks a series of questions around the age something is most likely to happen:

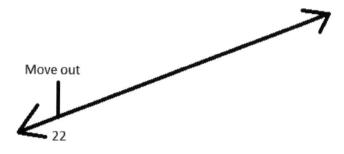

What is the age of people when they move out of their parents' home?

According to the joint Center for Housing Studies (Harvard/MIT), the peak age in the renter market is under 25 years old. The approximate peak age is 22 years old. (Keep in mind this and many of the peak ages of various statistical categories are moving northward, increasing naturally for the millennial and I generations, due to the fact the studies are ongoing and that some of the statistical categories will talk about this chapter are not well established for the millennial generation due to their youth.) We are going to concentrate on the previous generation's numbers: 22 years old. Logic would dictate this is when people are most likely to move out of their parents' home. People are either enrolled in college or skipping college and entering the workforce early. Either way, they need to be gainfully employed, amass a small amount of savings, and/or have enough income to move out, and do so in their early 20s.

Notable: Due to the massive accumulation of college debt, we assume that this peak age—and many of the peak age categories—will continue to increase as millennials and I generationers move into the typical patterns of purchases for the balance of their lives. This massive debt will likely delay inevitable purchases, specifically the year this generation starts to move out of the parents' homes.

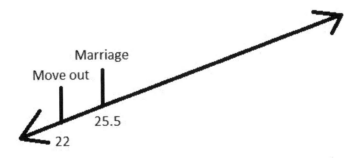

When do they get married?

The previous generation's peak age for marriage was 25.5 years old; the millennial generation's peak age is 28.2. The significance of this statistic matters to more of us than just the wedding caterers among us. According to authors Julian Simon and Stephen D. Moore, who wrote the book *It's Getting Better*

All the Time: 100 Greatest Trends of the Last 100 Years, "The best way to avoid poverty is to wait until after marriage to have children and to get married after 25 years old." If one were to do so, they would virtually eliminate all chance of poverty for the rest of their lives.

The increase in the marriage age is significant for the future, as it will likely increase the peak spending age of the millennial generation (more on this later). It is my belief that the reason the peak age of first marriage is increasing is as a result of two dynamics:

According to the former deputy director of the Central Intelligence Agency (CIA) Herb Meyer, in a presentation I attended, "As members of a society climb the socioeconomic ladder [in other words, make more money], they have fewer and fewer children, and all life events tend to happen later in life."

Due to the accumulation of debt and the financial crisis known as the Great Recession, millennial spending patterns—and therefore their life event time—has been delayed. Confirmation of this theory will establish itself in the next decade.

WHEN DO THEY HAVE THEIR FIRST CHILD?

The government statistics on first live births are startling. The main reason is that the overwhelming majority of research is done on unwed mothers, which is dictated by federal mandate. This is due to the fact that unwed, teenage mothers are highly detrimental to the economy as teenage births almost always lead to poverty for the new parents and as potential non-functioning members of society. Because of their negative effects on the nation, the government must keep an eye on their statistics. This muddies the research, as it moves the mean age currently in 2014 to 26.2 years old. This is younger than the start of marriage at 28.2. My belief is that this is because the federal government is very concerned about unwed mothers, specifically teenage pregnancies due to their direct connection to poverty.

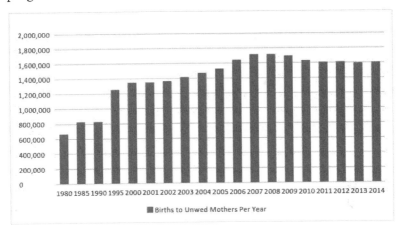

(Retrieved from the Center for Disease Control)

A total of 3,988,076 live births were registered in the United States in 2014, up 1 percent from 2013. The total fertility rate among women aged 15 to 44 rose in 2014 to 1862.5 births per 1000 women. This statistic is significant, because a society has to reproduce at least itself, requiring 2100 births per 1000 women, meaning the population would replace itself, give or take some unfortunate infant fatalities.

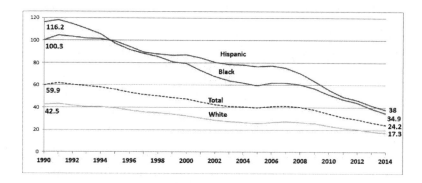

This data is ethnographic and not very useful for our purposes, but it does show that the trend of teenage births is negative, which is very good for our economy, in that poverty is less likely among families (i.e. married couples and non-teenage mothers).

The birth rate for teenage women aged 15 to 19 declined 9 percent from 2013 to 2014, which is a historical low for the nation. The birth rate declined to a record low for women in their early 20s in 2014; rates rose for women in their late 20s and early 40s from 2013 and 2014. The mean age of the mother at first birth rose again in 2014 to 26.3, up from 26 2013

The most troubling statistic is the birth rate for unmarried women. Although decreasing, the number is still staggering—the total births for unmarried women 2014 was 1,604,870 births. By my calculation that's 40.24 percent of all live births last year was to unmarried women. So what can we glean from the statistics?

Notables:

The millennial generation is waiting to get married, and millennial females are waiting the longest of any recorded generation to have their first child. This will ultimately move the magic age of millennial generation spenders away from the normal spending age for Gen. Xers and Boomers in the United States (more on that later).

Teenage pregnancies have steadily fallen, which is good for society, as children born to teenage mothers are more likely to live in poverty and need to be taken care of by society as opposed to being attentive and engaged citizens, according to Simon and Moore's *It's Getting Better All the Time: 100 Greatest Trends of the Last 100 Years*. One might argue that this drain on the economy will decrease as the number of teenage births decreases.

Millennial females are potentially the most at peace with having a child while unmarried or cohabitating. How this will play out for them and their financial lives is yet to be determined. This is not necessarily a bad thing, and if she's north of 25 years old everything might be fine depending on your social attitudes toward the institution of marriage.

I understand why the government is so enthusiastic about accumulating accurate statistics on teen pregnancies, and propagating initiatives to decrease these numbers in future generations, as they are the basis for most poverty in the United States. I can only assume that once we are able to extract married mothers from the data census, the mean age will increase from 26.2 to somewhere north of 28.2 years old, which is the peak age of marriage.

The reason why I am so interested in what the peak age is to have your first child while married or cohabitating is we can simply **add the peak age of first live birth to the peak age of when a human being moves out of their parents' home in order to figure out** when that parent is likely to peak as a spender. This formula would give us the peak spending age of the next generation, and then we can simply figure out how many people are turning that age and be able to tell the health of the economy decades in advance—which by now you should have figured out is the foundation for all strategic planning, marketing planning, and even financial planning.

FINANCED PURCHASES

There are macro trends that affect anything that is financed. For example, furniture, appliances, homes, real estate, and automobiles are all affected by macro trends, such as prevailing interest rates and access to capital, and all of these categories contribute to the peak of the purchases of these items.

So it is the combination of prevailing macro trends with predictable buying cycles that gives us our economic reality. Unfortunately, macro trends, such as interest rates and/or panic in the credit markets, are far less predictable. Fortunately, the buying cycles of normal human beings are ridiculously predictable.

At what age do they buy their first home?

The peak age of first-time homebuyers varies depending on the source of the information in the context of the study. I believe what would also muddy the analysis is what constitutes your definition of a starter home? Having said all of that, the range of first-time homebuyers is between 29 and 35 years old depending on category, for example, co-ops, condos, trailer homes, starter houses, etc.

I believe based on all the surveys and studies I've researched that we can safely say 31 years old is the peak age of first-time homebuyers.

Peak age of trade-up home purchases

According to Miriam Webster, trade up (verb): to trade something in (such as an automobile/house) for something more expensive or valuable of its kind.

It appears the peak in trade-up home purchases happens in one's early 40s. Logic would dictate this would be the case, as the first home purchase in the early 30s due to the need for shelter combined the birth of young children facilitates the whole the starter home purchase cycle. In the early 40s, as the size of said children increases, the requirement for space increases, coinciding with a significant increase in parental income, facilitating the dream home or trade-up home purchase cycle.

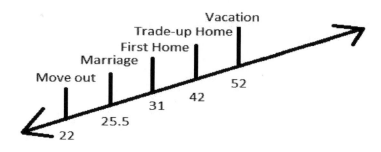

Peak age to purchase a vacation property

Based on my informal surveys and some research with the mortgage industry, the peak age to purchase a first-time vacation property or second home is in the early 50s. At the time of this writing, interest rates are at an all-time low, and the rate of second home purchases is up 57 percent, according to the mortgage industry. This might lead one to think that we're missing out and we better grab a vacation home to get in front of the curve. Given the fact that the peak year of boomer births was 1961—which means as of 2016, they are 55 years old—combined with the peak age for first-time second homes in the early 50s— the boom may have already passed. This, combined with the fact that interest rates are at an all-time low, gives one pause about jumping in with both feet. The timing could be wrong; many of the traits go higher and the demand diminishes naturally (because the peak age of people who purchase these properties are decreasing for the next 14 straight years.

Having said that, the age of purchasing the dream vacation home or second vacation home (i.e., oceanfront property) peaks in the late 60s, therefore the demand driving those real estate prices increases significantly as boomers become 55 years old into their late 60s. This gives one reason to think that this market will be in full-on growth mode for around the next 20 years despite what interest rates will do. This is similar to the way the condo/co-op/starter home market exploded in the 80s as baby boomers started to enter those peak ages. This dream vacation home property peaks right around the same time the classic retirement home "55 and over housing" and/or assisted-living facilities peak as people enter into those age brackets. Either of these two categories is likely to enjoy good decades ahead.

IN SUMMARY

The purpose of this chapter was to point out how predictable the average person is in the United States today. I used "shelter" to illustrate predictable buying patterns of the average person, given the fact that shelter is a basic human need.

The buying patterns in real estate are so predictable they border on boring and therefore do not make good fodder for newspaper articles and television stories. As the saying goes, "bad news is good news," i.e., "if it bleeds, it leads," and understanding this maxim helps us to understand the average person. In embracing how predictable the average person is that we can use these behavior patterns at certain times of our lives to predict industries decades in advance. In other words, the predictable buying patterns of human beings is the foundation all strategic planning, and knowledge of those patterns needs to be incorporated into all strategic plans. This can even be expanded to include marketing plans. Having said that, the two areas that this philosophy does not help to predict are, one, the whims of fashion and, two, the vagaries of economic forces such as currency fluctuation and interest rates.

Keep in mind, though, that if I could predict the whims of fashion and the vagaries of economic forces, I would be too busy counting my trillions to write this book. Although it is unfortunate that we cannot predict either of those two categories, the fact that we can predict the buying patterns of human beings decades in advance is better than not doing it.

CHAPTER 3

CHANGE THE LENS YOU SEE THE WORLD THROUGH

It is vital for a business to know the peak age of the end user of its product or service. This information is readily available, and in Chapter 5, we go through the peak spending patterns of as many categories as we possibly can. This chapter talks about how you can change the lens you view the world through—whether you are an investor, a business owner, or a government employee— in order to know which industries will thrive in the coming years. This chapter will help you become a better forecaster.

Let's pretend for a moment that you are a residential contractor, meaning you fix up homes for a living. Ask yourself how important would it be to know how many people are between the ages of 31 and 50 years old in your neck of the woods.

Game-changer important!

It's readily available and free.

Census Website Function:

www.census.gov/mycd/?eml=gd#

My Congressional District

(The census plays a role by being able to tell anybody how many people of a certain age live in any given congressional district in the United States.)

Which is more important, knowing the number of people in your neck of the woods that are of a certain age or the demographic trends (whether the number of people in one specific age group is increasing or decreasing) of those people?

I humbly submit to you that the trend is more important. Trends are more valuable due to the fact that as businesses attempt to expand, so do their expenses. So implementing a strategic plan can be very expensive. How do you know that your strategic plan is pointed in the right direction? If you don't understand your own marketplace, mastering the use of demographics for strategic planning is a path to a true understanding of your real marketplace. Any strategic plan that does not take into account demographics is a waste of time and planning to fail.

What should a business do if the trends are increasing (meaning, in the case of a residential contractor, the number of human beings turning 35 in the next 15 years)?

The universal answer in our surveys is to ramp up, meaning:

Buy out the competition

Invest in capital infrastructure

Advertise

Hire

Grow at virtually all costs

What should you do if the number of people turning 35 is decreasing for the next 15 years? When I ask this question in my workshops, I receive a host of answers, such as selling, downsizing, pull in the reins, etc. The best answer I received was from an architect in Brookfield, Wisconsin. The answer was not only shockingly good, but even more impressive is that it came from an architect.

When I asked the CEOs in attendance if they would ever let an architect run their company, the universal answer is no. Even the architects all answered no. There's usually an explicative in front of the word no. It would appear architects fall into two major categories:

The perfectionist, with the proverbial screws in too tight

The wacky artist who wants to win awards

Neither of which makes for an excellent CEO, but this architect with the snappy answers was the exception. For his answer to the question of decreasing target demographic, he said to "sell to someone that doesn't know that." It was the best answer I ever received, and he proceeded to answer about five more questions exceptionally well, to the point that I threw the marker down and accused him of not being an architect. If not, he was the worst architect I'd ever met. To that he stated with a smile on his face, "That's why I can run the company."

FROM MICROCOSM TO MACROCOSM

If we now step away from the local demographic world of the residential contractor and take a step into the larger economy, one where 49 ½ years old is the peak spending age of the average American and 55 years old starts the inevitable negative trend in spending (except in a few categories such as healthcare and the death industry).

This means we can expect a natural slowdown in consumer spending for most of the categories of industry, especially the areas that thrived in the past few decades.

In the mid-2000s, people would approach me at the end of my presentations with statements like, "Real estate is the best investment." I would then respond with, "Oh, yeah? Why's that?" They inevitably would say, "Because it goes up," I would then ask, "Why is that?" The responses, very typically, were, "Because it just does." Forget for a moment that the real estate market proved them wrong in the financial crisis of 2008 and understand that the lesson here is that if you don't know why a market is expanding, you will not know when or why it will contract in on itself.

The number of peak spenders in the United States started to decrease in mid-2011. But lucky for us, spending actually plateaus out to 55 years, so if we add 55 years old to the peak births in the United States in 1961-1962, this points to rough economic times starting in 2017 and lasting for 14 years. Given the dependency on her own consumer spending, it would appear that these trends are unavoidable for the United States.

WHY IS 49½ THE PEAK SPENDING AGE?

Although the Bureau of Labor Statistics can tell you the peak spending age of the average American, it cannot tell you why it is. So this next exercise is an attempt to reveal it through common sense.

In the previous chapter, we specified that the peak age to move out of a parent's home was 22 years old, and the peak age for first-time live births after marriage is 27. Logic would then dictate that if we simply added 22 years to 27, it would equal 49 years old. So we have determined through research and common sense that 49½ years old is the peak spending age because that is how old the parent is when the when the first child moves out. And because the child is the largest drain on the parents' money, they now are free to spend their surplus on whatever they feel like. This is also known as Empty Nester Spending Syndrome.

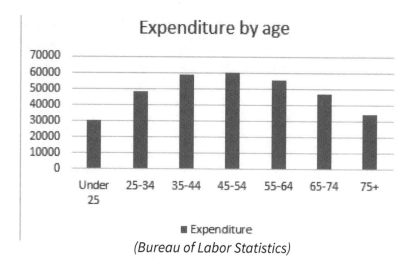

(Bureau of Labor Statistics)

So why is there a plateau out to 55 years old? The average family in America has two children. Fifty-five (although not always) is likely the year that the second child moves out. Logic dictates that due to this, this is the start of the natural decline in needs-based spending. As people stare at their own pending retirement, they change their spending to things such as health care and, if they can afford it, travel.

What do the parents do with the funds they would have spent on the children?

Judging from 401(k) deposits, I believe the first thing parents do, if they can, is increase investing in their retirement plans. I have the privilege of presenting to 401(k) trustees on average of four times a month, and they confirm these assumptions (their total responses bordering on empirical research).

I believe the second thing they do is start to pay down their credit card debt. This belief stems from formal research done with my clients.

Either case—paying down debt or investing in one's 401(k)—is not considered spending. Therefore, the aging of the baby boom generation and their inevitable empty nest syndrome does not bode well for the economy nor for consumer spending. We have a dichotomy: as the baby boomers start to spend less, naturally generation X cannot take over the mantle of spending because it is much smaller than the baby boom generation (Refer to the chart on births per year in the US).

It is not until the millennial generation starts to peak in spending, which is some 14 years later, that it can take over the mantle of spending much like its parent generation, the boomers.

WHAT, IF ANYTHING, CAN THE GOVERNMENT DO ABOUT THIS?

In order to move the needle on population numbers, the government (whichever government is applicable to you) has to be open to immigration. In Germany, the government has been increasingly open to Syrian refugees and immigrants from all over the world because they understand that immigration is the fuel that drives the economy. Most people do not realize that the last great wave of immigration into the United States came in 1990.

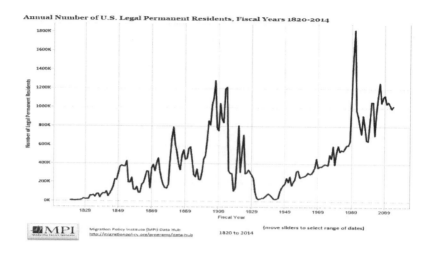

(Migrationpolicy.org)

US Department of Homeland Security offices of immigration statistics, Yearbook of immigration statistics.

Immigration- to come from somewhere else (to enter)

Emigration- to leave for somewhere else (to leave)

Migration- to move somewhere inside of a country

Knowledge of migration is especially important to states like Florida, as they need to understand how many people move there each day. For instance, Floridian engineers and city planners have taught me that currently there are 1001 people migrating to Florida each day. So, depending on your business it is important to understand these dynamics.

The peak age of immigration is 30 years old, and the last great wave of immigration was 1990. That would mean this massive wave of immigration, the peak numbers of whom were born in 1960, coincides with the peak in births of the baby boom generation. In other words, they are simply more generation Xers.

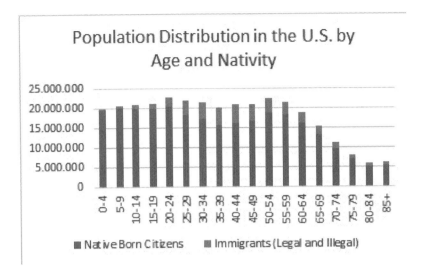

Source: Migration Policy Institute tabulation of data from the US Census Bureau's 2014 American Community Survey and 1970, 1980, 1990, and 2000 Census decennial data accessed from Steven Ruggles, J. Trent Alexander, Katie Genadek, Ronald Goeken, Matthew B. Schroeder, and Matthew Sobek, Integrated Public Use Microdata Series: Version 5.0 [Machine-readable database] (Minneapolis: University of Minnesota, 2010).

This chart displays the population of the US by age distribution and the population of immigrants, illegal and legal, compared to the native-born citizens. It clearly shows how immigrants to the US are picking up the slack in the spending of the generation Xers and will lessen the blow of the economic slump caused by the drop in the number of people in the magic spending age group.

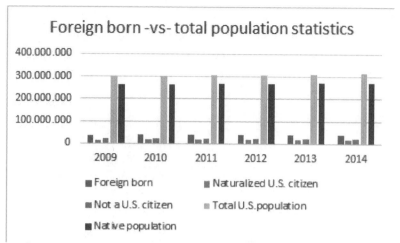

Foreign born -vs- total population statistics

Source: US Census Bureau, 2005-2009 American Community Survey

Currently there is a lot being made of Immigration, legal or otherwise, and its potential negative effects on our nation's economy. This appears to be much to do about nothing, especially when you see non-US native statistics compared the overall population. These are the latest stats as of the time of this writing: the native-born population grew by 12,645,551, or 4.19 percent, in the six years from 2009 to 2014, whereas the foreign-born population grew by 3,714,015, or 9.9 percent, over those same six years. The political firebrand stat currently is that as of 2014 illegal immigration was estimated to be 22,256,837 people.

A SHORT HISTORY OF IMMIGRATION

Immigrants, for all intents and purposes, peak in spending for the same reason as the rest of us. So this last great wave of immigration simply adds to the positive effects of the baby boom and does not exacerbate the negative effects. This does not solve the dead zone of spending, meaning the time period in which

Generation X could not support the amount of spending that the baby boomers had established.

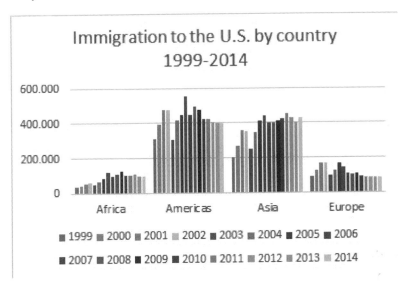

Source: http://www.migrationpolicy.org/sites/default/files/datahub/MPI-Data-Hub_USInflowLPRsbyCOB_2014.xlsx

If used correctly, one can put these statistics to use for future planning of the direction that their company will move towards. This will provide the glimpse at the future that is necessary for some very risky but profitable pivots in businesses everywhere. Demographics can be the theory that becomes the game changer in the lens one will see the world through.

CHAPTER 4

THE REAL GENERATIONS: WHO ARE THEY? AND HOW DO THEY LIVE?

This chapter outlines each of the generations relevant in the economy today. It outlines:

The generation

Its attitudes

Its education

Its health

Its housing

Its wealth

A common complaint from my CEOs is not understanding the millennial generation, but I believe if one were motivated enough, he or she could find countless references throughout history of the "current" generation complaining about the next up-and-coming generation.

"The past remembers better than it lived," highlighting the divide between reality and nostalgic, is attributed to the comedian Jackie Gleason by Simon and Moore in *It's Getting Better All the Time: 100 Greatest Trends of the Last 100 Years.* One of the underlying themes of this book is to dispel popular misbeliefs propagated by popular culture and the media. The authors describe how, right now, despite popular belief based on information sourced from the media, is the best time to ever be alive in world history. We are the healthiest, wealthiest people to ever walk the earth, especially in the US According to Simon and Moore, the human condition has historically been brutal and harsh, and life short, even just 117 years ago.

There are four basic assumptions I have about the media:

Whatever the camera focuses on fools us into thinking it's a larger representation of the whole.

Whatever gets repeated in the media tends to pull us into thinking it's happening more often than it is.

Bad news is good news, sometimes referred to as "if it bleeds, it leads"

What's in the best interest of the media is not necessarily in the best interest of the rest of us.

Science has advanced the study of how the mind works in the last 30 years at an astonishing rate. I've read all five of the best sellers on this subject, and they are listed below. I read between 30 and 50 books every year, and these books can make you wise rather than smart—because we all know that smart people can make crummy decisions.

How the Mind Works by Prof. Stephen Pinker (currently re-reading it, the best book I've ever read but a tough read)

Mindwise by Prof. Nicholas Epley

How Risky Is It Really? By television reporter David Ropeik (hilarious stories and proof that the evening news is a waste of one's time)

Thinking Fast and Slow by Nobel laureate Daniel Kanneman

The Science of Fear by journalist, Dan Gardner (a fantastically easy read and proof that the news industry is in full decline)

I believe our efforts should be focused on understanding the factual differences between the generations so that we can better understand our next employee and our next customer, in particular, the generational differences in education and attitudes.

EDUCATIONAL DIFFERENCES

Each of the generations born after World War II is increasingly educated. The world currently supports more higher thinkers today than ever before in world history, and the next up-and-coming generations are the most educated in American history. Once exclusively the realm of nobility, education is now available to the general population in developed countries, which was not the case in the Middle Ages.

Education affects attitudes and values, and therefore each younger generation behaves differently from that of their parents' generations. Add in a healthy dose of technological advancements, and behavior differences between generations are exaggerated all the more.

Important note: My opinion differs from most demographers and that of the Bureau of Labor Statistics. The Bureau of Labor Statistics cited that each generation starts and ends on what appears to be an arbitrary date. This research would be better served if we simply name the generation based on the trough peak cycles age wave. For example, the Bureau of Labor Statistics and the Census Bureau have decided that the increase in births leading up to World War II should be called the swing generation. I feel this needlessly complicates things, and if we name the generation from its trough to its peak, the swing generation is just the initial phase of the baby boom generation. This is more than just semantics and can lead to needless confusion, for example, a common statement here is that the millennial generation is larger than the baby boom generation, when in fact they were originally called the echo boom, as they are in effect the same size as the baby boom generation.

If you were to study the history of the age waves and their names, you would understand that these names change over time. I believe they were misnamed simply because they have to be named something, and then maybe that sticks and is useful but just because the Bureau of Labor Statistics decided to name the first wave of the baby boom generation the swing generation doesn't make it useful. Another way of naming the generations is from their trough to their peak, which helps us to do what we set out to in studying demographics, meaning to use them to predict spending, therefore, by extension, to use demographics to predict economic boom and bust periods. I believe naming them peak to trough is far more useful, so, therefore, for the remainder of the book, I will be using my own names for each generation.

For our purposes the generations are as follows:

THE WWII GENERATION, BORN PRIOR TO 1933

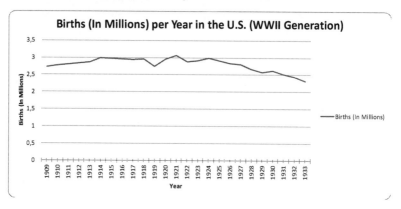

The WWII generation was shaped by the Great Depression and World War II to become the most religious and financially conservative of all the generations currently. This generation is currently fraught with health issues. Some 48 percent have at least one form of a physical difficulty, and 53 percent have arthritis. Cancer claims more lives in the middle years, but heart disease remains the leading killer of older adults.

THE BABY BOOM GENERATION, BORN 1933 TO 1962

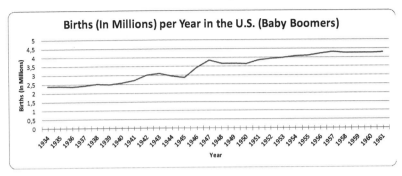

Births (In Millions) per Year in the U.S. (Baby Boomers)

The baby boom generation started the spending wave studies because of its sheer size in comparison to the previous generation. This led to the "Pig in the Python Theory": a sharp statistical increase represented as a bulge in an otherwise level pattern, used especially with reference to the baby boom generation regarded as having a gradual effect on consumer spending, society, etc. as it grows older. The baby boom generation became the obsession of advertisers and sociologists alike. After the soldiers returned from World War II, they settled down with their G.I. Bill and had a lot of children. This resulted in expansion, or what I would call the second wave of the baby boom generation. The government expects this sort of thing following wars. What they did not expect was that this expansion would Last another 19 years, resulting in the largest generation in American history. Or that this enormous generation would ultimately transform the American economy, culture, and in effect define the art of demography, which is a relatively new science/art.

The baby boom generation will be the future of:

The "empty nest" industry

The health care industry

The death industry

The elder industry (elder law, estates)

GENERATION X, BORN ROUGHLY BETWEEN 1962 IN 1976

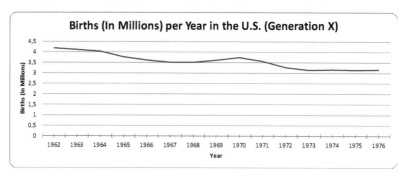

Previously known as the baby bust generation, or the forgotten generation, this generation marks the decrease in births starting in 1962 through in 1976. It showcases a prevalent sense of being overshadowed by the previous generation, as the media and advertisers paid infinitely more attention to the far larger baby boomers cohort. Considering the fact that this generation is sandwiched between two much larger generations, it is also likely to lead to challenges like "the great buyer's market ahead." More businesses will change hands in the next 15 years than ever before in American history. The dilemma will become who the baby boomers will sell their businesses to.

In 2016, there was approximately 50 million people in generation X; that represents approximately 20 percent of the population. Although the smallest of all recent generations, gen X represents the family-oriented, child-rearing generation, and much like the baby boom generation, they "live to work."

There are two potential effects of this on the economy:

Consumer spending dries up instantly, as the small Generation Xers cannot compensate for the difference in size of the boomers.

It will be crucial for companies to know how to pivot in order to cater to their new customers, the millennials and Gen. Xers, to make up for the losses in revenue.

THE MILLENNIAL GENERATION, BORN 1976 TO 1990

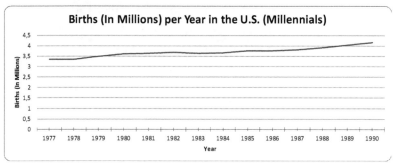

Births (In Millions) per Year in the U.S. (Millennials)

Once referred to as the Echo Boom, generation Y, it represents the children of the baby boomer, as the boomers had approximately two children and replicated themselves. Although they are the offspring of the baby boom generation, there are vast differences between these two generations

According to the previously mentioned author Julie Lythcott-Haims, after "America's Most Wanted" became the number-one television show in America, parenting changed from the latchkey, self-starter baby boom generation and the generation X to become ultimately taxi drivers and program directors for the millennials. This change in parenting resulted in frustration for employers of the millennial. Unlike their parents, who lived to work, the millennials want work to be fun.

This conundrum illustrates the age-old frustration of parents claiming that this generation just doesn't do things correctly. I believe this scenario has played out over eons of time as most generations scoff at the next one. Boomers/gen X business owners bemoan the state of hiring, which represents the number one challenge in my survey of Vistage CEOs. But I believe boomer/gen X CEOs are missing the point. Yes, millennials were over-parented due to overblown threat perception by their parents. But in this challenge is the seed of opportunity.

Millennials need direction, and boomers and gen Xers are excellent at giving direction. This could be a match made in heaven for a savvy boomer or gen Xer looking to form teams.

THE I GENERATION, OR 1990 TO 2007

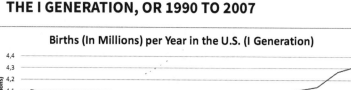

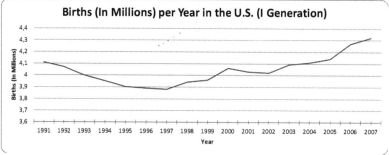

Births (In Millions) per Year in the U.S. (I Generation)

Given the fact that the name of generation X has changed twice and the name millennials has changed three times, I can only assume that this I generation moniker is temporary.

This digitally native generation grew up with the Internet, and its identity is still forming, but as a father of four generation I boys, I've observed that they seem remarkably similar to the millennial generation, with many needing direction. We shall see what attitudes and tastes they will develop. As of the time of this writing, the oldest of the I generation is merely 25 years old. The coming decades will shape and reveal their tastes and tendencies.

ATTITUDINAL DIFFERENCES

Results from the latest government surveys have shown that the presumed rebellious nature of the baby boom generation was exaggerated and that generation I is much more conservative than previously assumed. The millennial generation, by contrast, is far more liberal. The assumption is that attitudes change as we age—we become more conservative—but it appears, based on recent survey results, that attitudes are shaped in our youth and rarely change throughout our lives. Thus, it would appear that our attitudes are more concrete than previously thought. If these results hold true, we can expect America to become even more tolerant in the coming decades.

THE MEDIA IS IN FOR A CHANGE

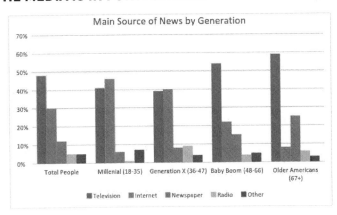

All graphs from the US Bureau of Labor Statistics

According to Daniel Gardener, author of *The Science of Fear: How the Culture of Fear Manipulates Your Brain,* we are graduating the fewest numbers of journalists in the history of journalism and the most news outlets ever. This is a troubling statistic for the media, as competition for views is so great that the truth is clouded in the fever of competition, greatly reducing popular media's credibility. Millennials and the I generation have already adopted the Internet for most things news. I can foresee a tipping point when the public turns a jaded eye to all news.

RELIGIOUS CHANGE

Millennials showcase less absolute belief in God. In the WWII generation, 70 percent believe absolutely in God, whereas, with millennials only 46 percent believe.

Protestant beliefs are in steep decline, all other major religions are in slight decline, whereas the only religion that seems to be holding its own is Catholicism, which holds the same numbers as it had with previous generations.

OPTIMISM AND TRUST

The sobering state is that millennials tend not to trust other human beings. A full 70 percent of millennials state that others are not trustworthy, as compared to 56 percent of baby boomers, who say they feel others are not trustworthy.

When asked are you happy, the majority say they are, and the numbers are consistent throughout all age groups.

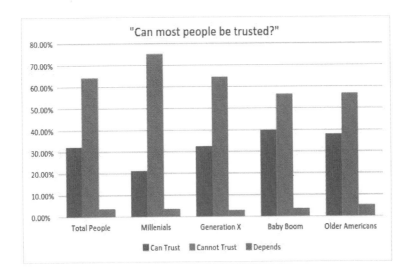

EDUCATION

The majority of millennials and I generationers at least start college, and about one-third finish with at least a baccalaureate degree.

"A bachelor's degree is like a high school diploma." — attributed to a frustrated millennial looking for work and preparing to go back to school.

Success depends on regularly reinventing one's self, which bodes extremely well for the education industry. The bachelor degree is slowly but surely becoming the bare minimum. Starting with generation X, each of the following generations are the most educated ever in the history of the United States.

HEALTH

Americans are the healthiest humans to ever walk the earth. Although, in this sense, health is defined in comparison with the many millennia of humans past. A man dying of starvation 10,000 years ago was not concerned with how much cholesterol or gluten was in his bread. The obesity crisis in the United States is a reality, yet human beings are the healthiest they've ever been due to the advancements in modern medicine. However some young will still die by accident, and the old lead in all cancer and heart disease statistics. Debate over health care is only just beginning, as the only two categories that have experienced inflation in costs in the last 20 years are college education and healthcare costs. If healthcare costs continue to escalate, the baby boom generation, as it ages, has the potential to bankrupt the Medicaid system and, by extension, dozens of states. Look for this to be a political hot-button issue in the coming decade.

Health statistics of note from the US Bureau of Labor Statistics:

40 percent of first-time mothers are not married (an all-time high)

The number of first-time live births to teenage mothers is at an all-time low

The majority of Americans are overweight

The majority of Americans do not get enough exercise

AMERICANS ARE LIVING LONGER

HOUSING

Home ownership peaked in 2004 and fell sharply in the financial crisis. The financial crisis affected the generations differently, but as a result, millennials are more likely to rent and are slow to adopt home ownership as a means of financial security, whereas the older generations' financial securities depended on their mortgage status.

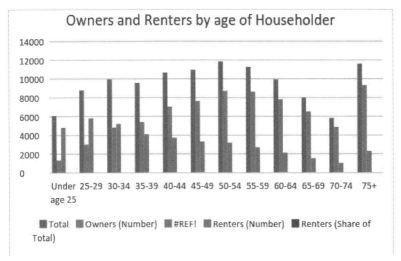

Migration versus Immigration

The young are more likely to move; the old are more likely to move far. The financial crisis put migration rates at an all-time low. The inability to sell a home left even the unemployed stuck, whereas in the past they would have simply sold their house and relocated for their careers. The inability to sell a home also affected natural migration patterns for empty nesters.

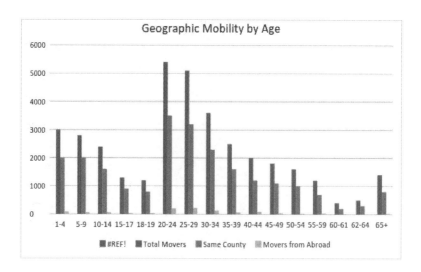

Income and the Decades of No Growth

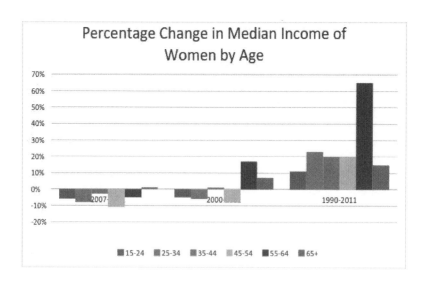

The Income Gap is Narrowing, Especially among the Young

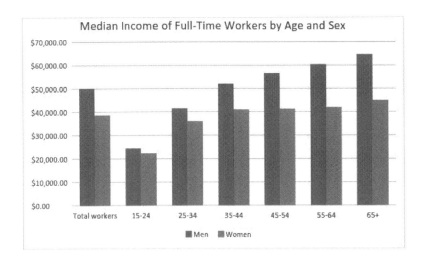

Americans Aged 45-54 Are Most Likely to Be Affluent

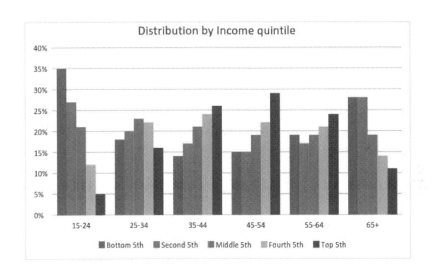

Income Peak in Middle Age Regardless of Race

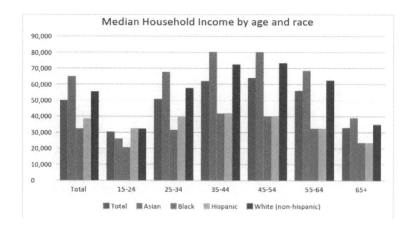

Asians report higher average income of any ethnicity, but in each category of age, the middle ages are the most prosperous out of all the age groups regardless of ethnicity.

MOST MOTHERS WORK

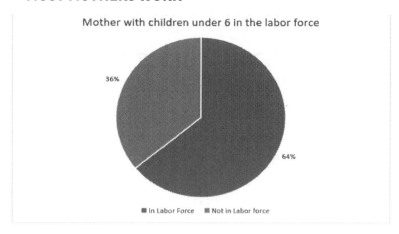

Marital Status

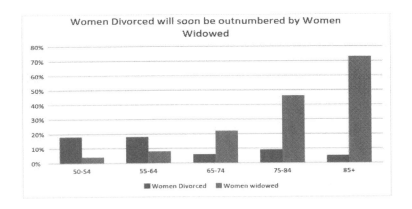

As the boomers age, women widowed will eventually outnumber women divorced. Younger generations are staying single longer.

DIVORCE STAYS STRONG

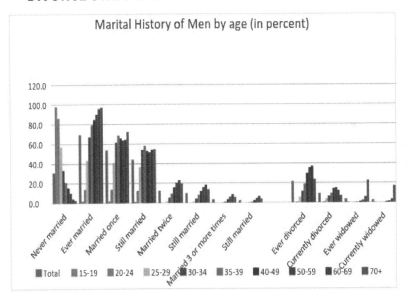

POPULATION PROJECTION

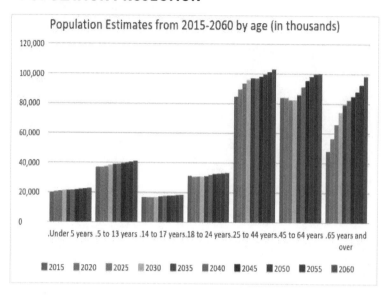

Population Estimates from 2015-2060 by age (in thousands)

MINORITIES WILL SOON OUTNUMBER THE MAJORITY

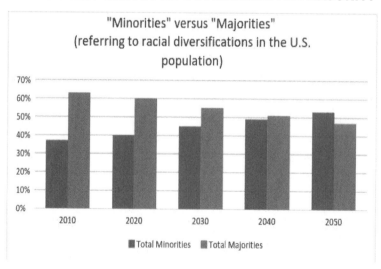

"Minorities" versus "Majorities" (referring to racial diversifications in the U.S. population)

POPULATION BY AGE AND PLACE OF BIRTH, 2011

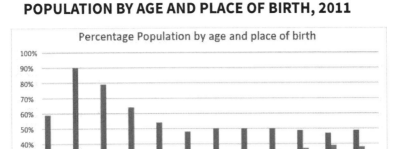

Only 13% of the population was born outside the US Most immigrate to the US looking for work. By age, the largest proportion of foreign-born is found among people aged 23.

STATE POPULATION BY AGE

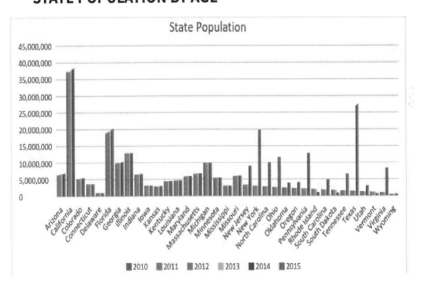

WEALTH

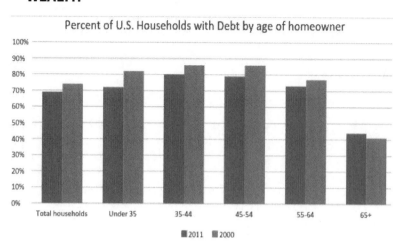

Percent of U.S. Households with Debt by age of homeowner

WEALTH AND ASSET DISTRIBUTION BY AGE

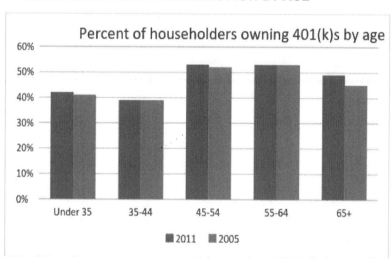

Percent of householders owning 401(k)s by age

CHAPTER 5

THE DEMOGRAPHICS OF CONSUMER DEMAND AND YOUR NEXT CUSTOMER

This chapter outlines the peak spending patterns of every studied industry. For example:

Alcohol

Apparel

Computers

Entertainment

Financial services

Furnishings and equipment

Gifts

Groceries

Healthcare

Household services

Housekeeping supplies

Personal care

Reading material

Restaurants

Shelter

Telecommunications

Tobacco

Transportation

Travel

Utilities

Spending and lifestyle are undoubtedly linked. I believe the changes in fashion are near impossible to predict, but the lifestyle spending of the average American does not hinge on fashion, it hinges on a highly predictable life pattern, which inevitably shows up as statistical norms in lifestyle spending. Predicting the trends in spending becomes easy when one includes common sense. For example, common sense would dictate spending on health care increases directly with age. Other categories of spending are not quite so obvious. The information in this chapter is designed to help you forecast trends in spending. This chapter is based on data collected by the US Census Bureau, Bureau of Labor Statistics, the National Center for Education Statistics, and the National Center for Health Statistics. For example, the Census Bureau has a current population survey, a survey that it conducts every month of more than 60,000 households.

The Bureau of Labor Statistics consumer expenditure survey, or the CEX, is the cornerstone for predicting spending on products and services. The CEX is an ongoing study of large expenditures, such as cars, as well as day-to-day purchases, such as hygiene products. The information contained in the survey and the statistics/data the Bureau produces is, for our purposes, invaluable to all industries studied. However, the only challenge of the CEX is that it is passive, meaning the participants in the survey, through their responses, show where they have spent money. This makes requests for specific information for each industry passive, as opposed to being able to study one category of industry over another.

For example, the government has no particular reason to push for more intensive studies on office products over furniture. This means that there will be less information on a particular industry than something the government needs to keep tabs on, such as teenage pregnancies. For specific industry information, you can turn to that specific industry's trade association, and if that doesn't satisfy your need for research, you can go the more expensive route of market research companies.

Another complication is that the studies done on purpose are usually done by federal mandate, usually gathering important information on the more dangerous aspects of spending, i.e., teenage first-time births, not necessarily providing great value for the less dangerous. Given the fact that these the surveys and studies are less than perfect for everything we need, they still suggest valuable trends, and we can gather what to expect in future trends. For example, baby boomers are likely to postpone retirement age, which can change the peak spending age of the average American as a result. We have discovered through the use of the CEX that the boomers are peaking in their earning years and, thus, they may actually be able to change the peak spending age if they continue to work.

Millennial spending patterns, on the other hand, are dramatically affected by the bloated student loan debt, which has an effect on spending, affecting all statistical categories, for example, when they are likely to move out, peak in spending, etc. In other words, their buying patterns are more likely to happen later in life. This may explain why the peak age of marriage has been extended over the last 15 years. This dynamic will likely affect every statistical category of spending potentially even delaying the peak age of spending, which is so critical to predicting the economies the future.

HEALTHCARE SPENDING CHART

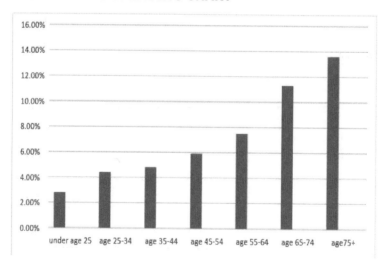

This might seem obvious, but healthcare spending increases proportionally as a person ages. I have found that the last 90 days of a person's life are so expensive that if you were to add up the expenses of the rest of your life compared to the last 90 days, they would be approximately equal.

Healthcare is a recession-resistant category due to the age wave, i.e., as baby boomers age, they or their loved ones will always spend more on healthcare and, as a result, this industry will do well regardless of the economic cycle.

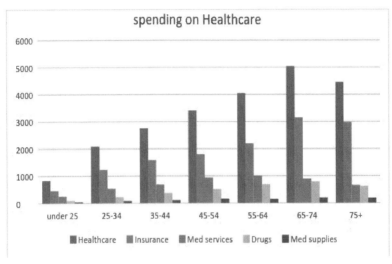

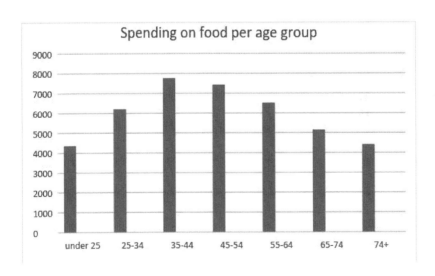

Fourteen years old is the peak age for calorie intake due to the fact that this is a period of rapid growth for pubescent teenagers, who require a lot of energy in the form of food. If the peak age of those having live births is 26 to 30-year-olds, it would hold true that 35 to 44 would make up the majority of spending in the food industry because they have hungry teenagers living at home who are in need of the most food they will ever eat in their entire lives.

APPLICATION

The census can actually help restaurants, grocery stores, etc. as through understanding census data market strategists can know the average age of every person on every block in the United States.

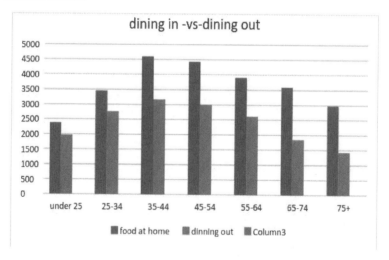

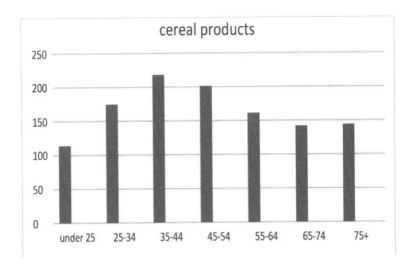

For example, cereal's success depends on the amount parents of teenagers are willing to spend on cereal compared to something else. The more 35-to-44 year-olds there are, the better cereal products will do due to the sheer amount of demand provided by teenagers. The same goes for bakery, meat, dairy, or any other food product sold in a grocery store.

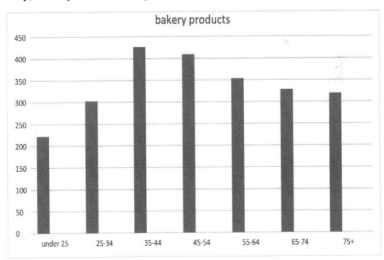

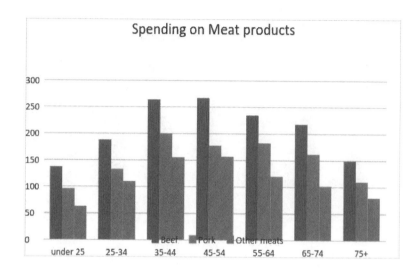

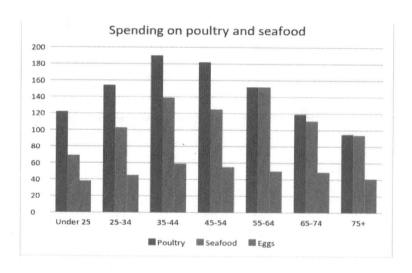

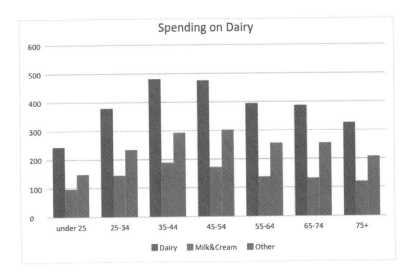

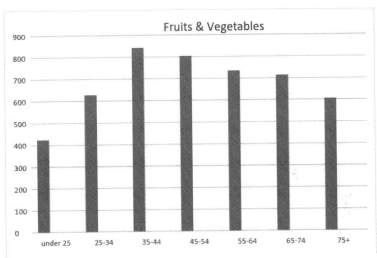

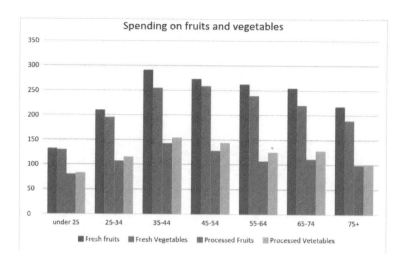

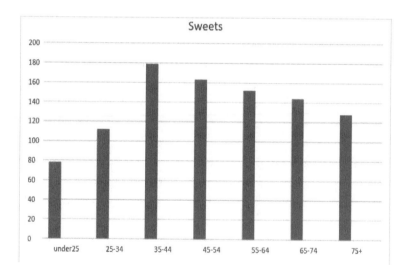

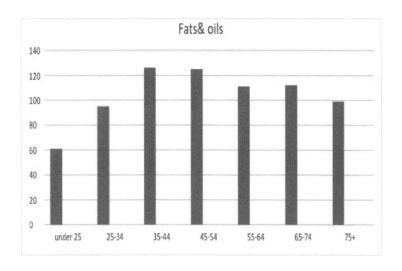

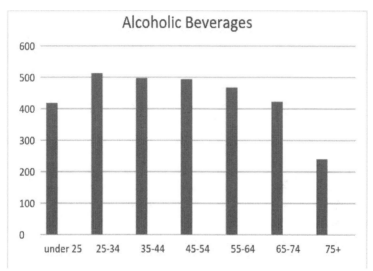

On tap? Spending on alcohol varies by age group and the fashion of the day. It appears that Americans love to unwind with their favorite beverage. Trends: beer overall is losing market share to wine and liquor. Boomer spending, according to Nielsen research, appears flat for the past decade. Look for the switch to more sophisticated drinks, although beer will remain the most popular of all beverages. Look for tastes to change as boomers and millennials make the switch to quality, i.e., blended scotch to single malt and stock beers to craft beers, as they are the more quality choice. Spirits and wine are going to expand in the "off-premise" categories, meaning into bars and restaurants.

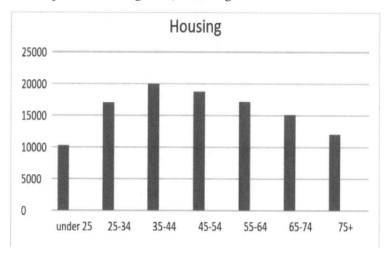

It would appear caloric intake is connected the housing ladder as a generation climbs that ladder. Meaning, as children grow, so does their food intake, and as they grow in size, so should their shelter size. Thus, spending on housing parallels spending on food.

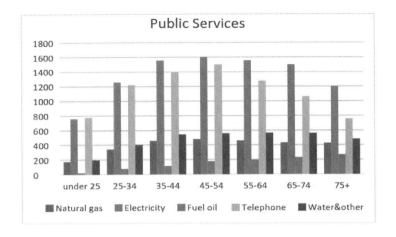

Typically a recession-resistant business model, according to Maslow's Hierarchy of Needs, utilities or "needs"-based spending increases up till age 35, then levels off, but stays essential, as all people need water and heat to live. Look at these utilities as a diversification tool, as this industry tends to be recession resistant.

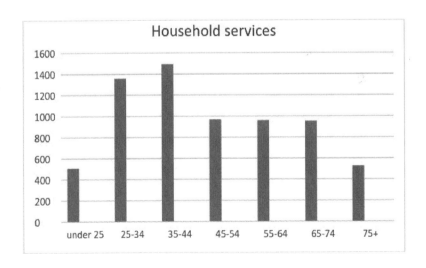

Household services refers to such activities as cleaning a house, childrearing activities, maintaining lawns, making repairs to household appliances, and so forth. This is a useful service but it is not recession-resistant, as it is a luxury service that is not placed in the same ballpark as food, water, heat, and shelter.

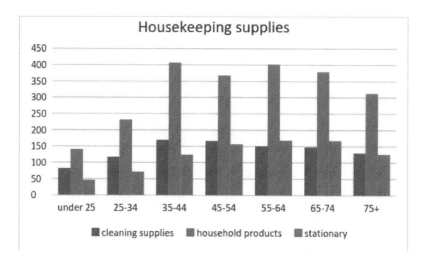

Cleaning supplies are always in demand, as people need cleaning supplies regardless of the economic cycle. And because they're so cheap it is worth it.

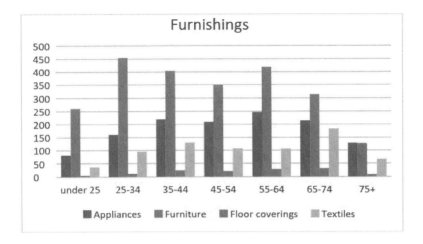

Furnishings appear to have a double peak: 25 to 34 years and 55 to 64 years old are the two peak spending ages for furnishings. This makes sense, as the fashion of the day might win out when finding a home that needs restoration or renovation once the buyers have become empty nesters. Not to mention that the fashions that once looked great might look horrendous 25 years later. Bad 70s fashions now come to mind.

This category might be better represented if we split the stats between men and women, as men's and boy's spending is a minority, only attaining two-thirds as much as their same-age female counterparts and dropping to half as much at their peak years. The relatively small generation X is hurting sales in this category currently. Look for this to revive as millennials grow into the older age groups and fill in this gap.

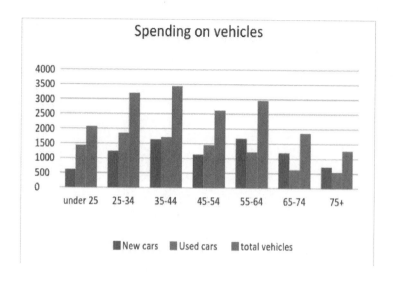

Spending on new cars peaks at 55 to 64; spending on used cars peaks at 25 to 34 years old. Interestingly, spending on used cars wanes after 44 years old. This category should be subject to further analysis as to why the total revenue for total vehicles sold changes as the number of millennials increase the category of 44 to 54 years in the next decade.

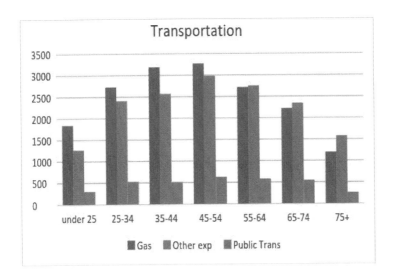

This category certainly confirms that we are a car-crazed country. Gas and other expenses easily outweigh spending on public transportation and peak in the 45 to 54 year range, with public transportation being relatively constant throughout life.

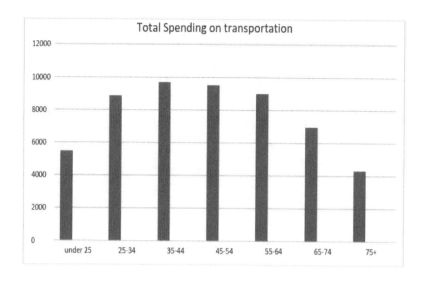

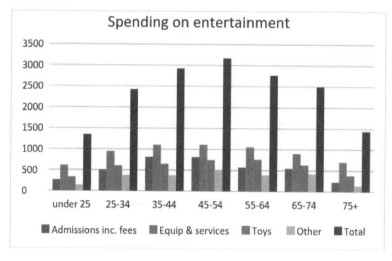

Although spending on entertainment peaks at 45 to 54 years old, spending on admission and fees peaks and level off at 35 to 64 and on.

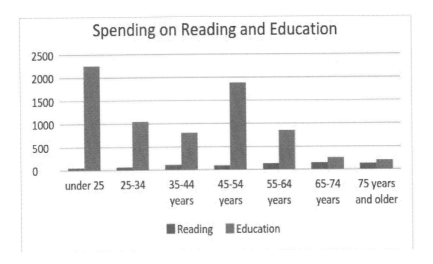

Education spending seems to have a double peak, one at 25 and under and another at 45 to 54 years. This is obviously due to the fact that most people go to college and have to deal with student loans under age 25, and at the ages of 45 to 54 parents, usually begin sending their children off to college and help foot their bills. Reading seems to peak at 35 to 44 and levels out from then on.

CHAPTER 6

COUNTERCYCLICAL DEMOGRAPHIC COUNTRIES AND HOW TO UTILIZE THIS INFORMATION

This chapter gets into which countries will thrive just as the US economy starts to decline. This is a diversification strategy for investors and business owners alike. You will understand what other markets you need to diversify into, whether as an investor or manufacturer. This chapter defines an international diversification tool and teaches you how to use it to your advantage.

The most useful tool to begin with is The World Factbook CIA: https://www.cia.gov/library/publications/the-world-factbook/fields/2010.html

The CIA is unbelievably forthcoming with its data, and as a result, I have been able to find the population of every specific age group in every country in the world that is significant to my purposes (investing, outsourcing, etc.) Although I have to assume the CIA has different purposes for this data, nonetheless it is incredibly useful and important.

DIVERSIFICATION BY UTILIZING THE INDUSTRIALIZED WORLD

Austrian political leader Klemens von Metternich (1773–1859) once said, "When France sneezes, the world catches a cold." Although originally referring to France, it is more appropriate today to apply this to the United States.

WE SNEEZE, AND THE WORLD CATCHES A COLD

What is meant by this? The US is a net importer, and the evidence to support this claim is the massive trade deficit we have with the rest of the world. This means that as we go, so goes the rest of the world. So if we either accelerate or decelerate in spending, the rest of the world feels the effects. You'll see from the rest of this chapter that the majority of the industrialized world has demographic trends similar to that of the United States. This, in turn, exaggerates the positive effects of spending or exacerbates the negative impact of lack of spending depending on whether we are in a boom or bust cycle.

I have mentioned that there is no economy in the world more dependent on its own consumer spending than the United States. When our economy starts its natural decline, this will wildly effect the world economy, causing worldwide economic doldrums. The "natural decline" will be a result of the lack of births between 1962 and 1976, also known as generation X. This means fewer people will be peaking in spending for the next 15 years, which leads to a drop in GDP and, as a result, the US sneezes and the world catches a cold.

I am making the assumption that not all economies had a "baby boom," and some of those that did might have countercyclical (to the US) demographic trends, such as Japan, which could be used as a diversification tool. The effectiveness of consumer spending as a projection tool is less effective in other countries because most are net exporters and do not have the dependency on consumer spending to the same degree as the United States.

Diversification strategies for CEOs and investors:

There are countries we can sell into that will be coming into their own boom as we start to slow down.

Investing in international companies that would be immune to the effects of the downturn due to countercyclical demographics can help you save what you would have lost while you wait out the storm.

So when we start our slowdown, this will affect net exporters the most, and only a few of them have a countercyclical demographic trend similar to ours. Those that do can rely on their population's power to spend to keep their economies afloat, or at least lessen the burden.

I'd like to showcase the Japanese economy first, as it has the strongest countercyclical trend to the United States. The majority of my formative years were spent listening to how great their economy was; this was attributed to the way the Japanese did business rather than sound fundamentals.

NIKKEI INDEX

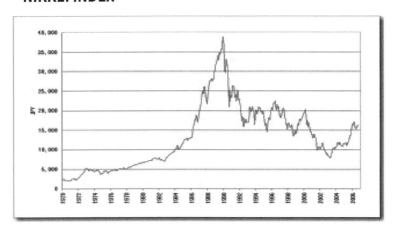

Source: Nikkei.org

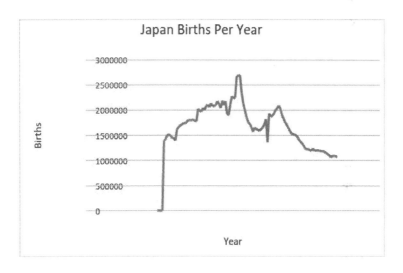

Source: Japanese Ministry of Health, Labor, and Welfare

From 1985-1989, the Nikkei Index (basically, the Japanese DOW JONES) had grown by 100 percent per year for four years, growing from 10,000 to about 40,000 points. My college advisors were telling students, including myself, to "go back to school as an international finance major and learn Japanese." This seemed sound advice, as the Japanese had outgrown us (in growth rate, never in size) for 30 years. We were told it was the way they did business:

» Lifetime employment

» Worker bee mentality

» Decision by committee

These were actually cited as the reasons why the Japanese economy grew so much so fast. These assumptions have all been disproven in the 27 years since. The Nikkei Index fell in 1989-2002 from approximately 40,000 to 7000; this became known as the "lost two decades." Worse yet, the real estate market in Japan, which had been a phenomenon, peaked in 1990. At the time, the island of Japan was estimated to be worth 4 times the entirety of the United States. In fact, the Japanese started to buy up parts of the US, including parts of Hawaii, Rockefeller Center, and Pebble Beach, just to name a few. It was considered less expensive to buy US property than to buy Japanese. In fact, the Japanese real estate boom got so out of hand, the Japanese had to invent the 100-year mortgage to enable the average Japanese citizen to afford a home.

Unfortunately, the market turned and real estate prices collapsed, as it became legal to indenture future generations. In a recent Vistage presentation, one member, who was married to a Japanese national, stated, "In Japan, they no longer consider real estate an appreciating asset, they consider it a depreciating asset," which represents a massive paradigm shift.

I believe there are two reasons for this shift:

The neighboring countries (China, South Korea, Vietnam, etc.), with their access to natural resources and cheap labor, out-produced and stole markets from the Japanese.

Once the Japanese lost their competitive advantage, the spending at home could not save them because they were a nation of old people, and old people do not like to spend money.

Despite virtually every economic stimulus program, the Japanese spent two decades in what could be referred to as a Depression.

Utilizing age/demographic information from the CIA, we can understand and even predict which countries around the world will have booming economies and which will have busting economies. Personally, I believe this can be incredibly valuable information with regard to diversification strategies. From expanding into new markets or diversifying investment strategies, mastering the information in the following pages will go a long way toward producing your best strategic plan.

POPULATION PYRAMIDS ON PAST AND FUTURE ECONOMIC POWERHOUSES:

THE AMERICAS

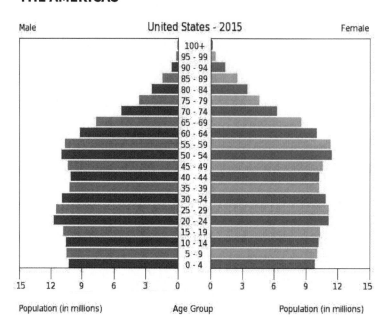

The number of people turning 55 decreases in the next 15 years, which will have a negative effect on consumer spending. Spending dries up as we age and as we become empty nesters. This will badly affect US Gross Domestic Product (GDP) as a whole. But depending on our immigration policies, we may be able to prevent this oncoming economic um.

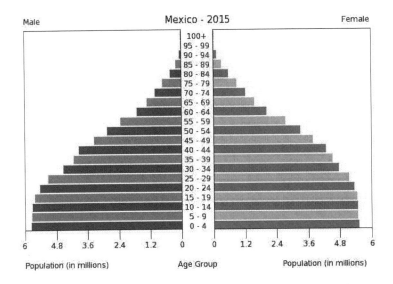

Mexico's economy will flourish in the next few decades, building up to a massive peak in spending when the largest population bracket now turns 55 then. Mexico is preparing to be a new economic juggernaut and probably one of the world's top economies in the coming years.

Keep in mind that young people do dumb things like doing drugs, joining gangs, and overall violence. Know that the media will show the negatives that come along with a large population of youths, however the news will not display the economic boom that comes from such a demographic. Do not rely on the news for help making investment decisions.

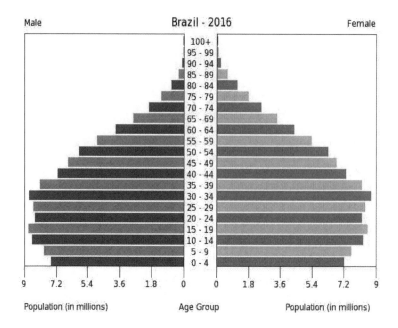

Male   **Brazil - 2016**   Female

Brazil will be very similar to Mexico in terms of economic prosperity. They are just as bullish and will also be one of the top economies soon enough.

The only thing that gives me pause is their protectionist policies. This will likely limit their growth and make them difficult to do business with. They will definitely experience an upward economic shift, just not nearly as much as if they were trade friendly.

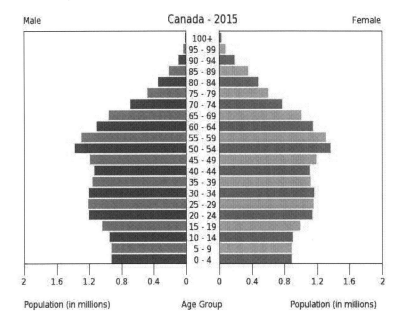

Canada cannot be accurately represented by this chart due to its economic reliance on oil rather than consumer spending. Information on Canada's economy will be found in a chart of expected future oil prices.

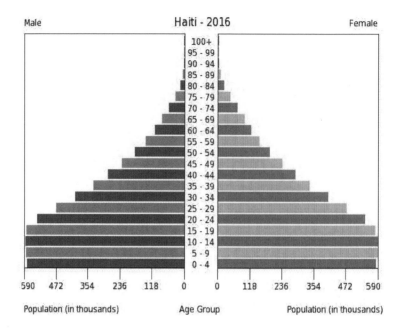

Haiti will do surprisingly well, but shows signs of bearishness in 2056.

NORTHERN EUROPE

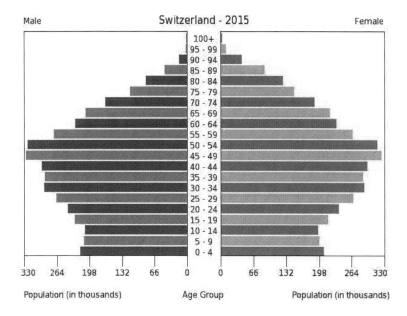

The number of people turning 49 to 59 may be high at the moment, but in the coming years, Switzerland's economy will not do nearly as well as it is doing now. Switzerland will have to depend mainly on immigration for economic prosperity.

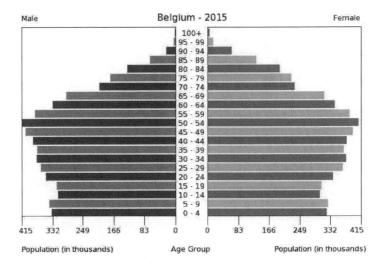

Male Belgium - 2015 Female

Population (in thousands) Age Group Population (in thousands)

Similar to the Swiss, the Belgian population of 50-year-olds will decrease over the next 40 years. I would not expect them to be a flourishing economy and the likelihood is that they would have to import immigrants, to support their tax base, from countries with a countercyclical trend to their own.

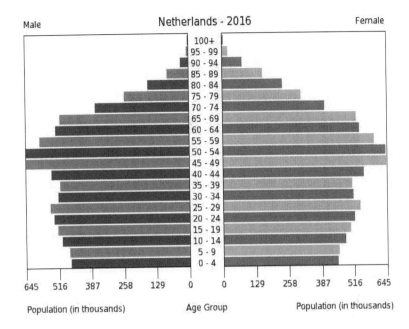

The Dutch population, like the majority of Europe, decreases each year except for a minor number of 30-year-olds. The Netherlands will have to import a tax base in the form of immigration. Do not look for diversification or investment opportunity in this economy. The only strategy that will help is mastering the art of exporting to countries that will be in growth mode.

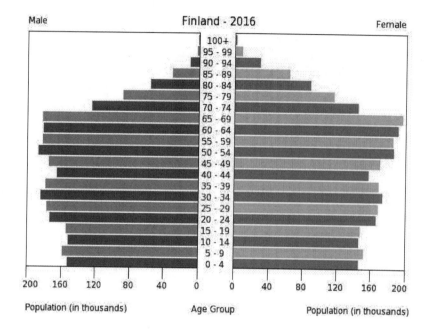

Finland has peaked and will remain with this trend beyond the forecastable future.

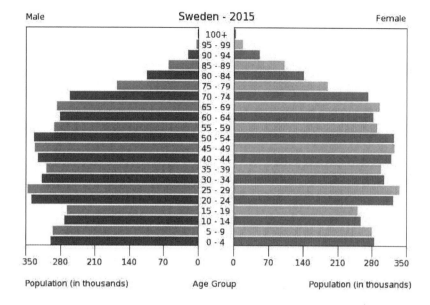

Although the Swedish population chart undulates, there are plenty of young people in Sweden compared to the rest of Europe. Sweden will have a nice bounce-back in the population of 30-year-olds. Projection will be up and down for the next 40 years depending on their immigration policies.

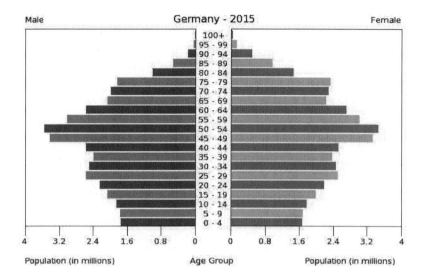

Germany is very bearish and will have some tough times ahead if they are not willing to let immigrants into their country. Based on current behavior patterns towards immigrants this bodes well for their economy in the future and I would suggest continuing accepting attitudes towards immigrants.

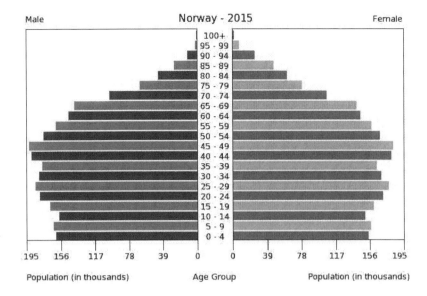

I have a very bearish view of Norway, and at the time of this writing, oil prices are half of what they used to be. The peak spending age is 49; this age decreases every year, but it is not a huge decrease] Similar to the rest of Europe, Norway will be in slow decline. I advise against any investments besides those targeting export-focused countries.

WESTERN EUROPE

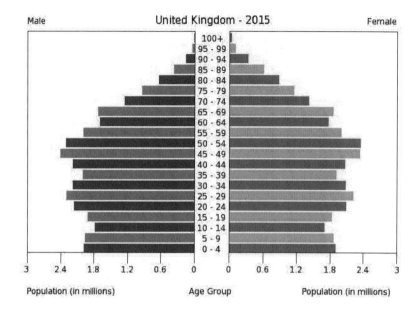

The UK will go through a similar economic experiences as the US.

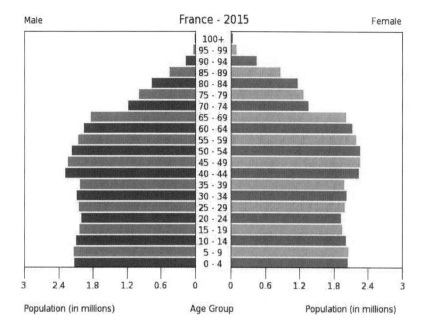

France remains neutral, neither boom nor bust for the next 40 years. They have peaked already and will continue with a similar trend for the next 50 or so years.

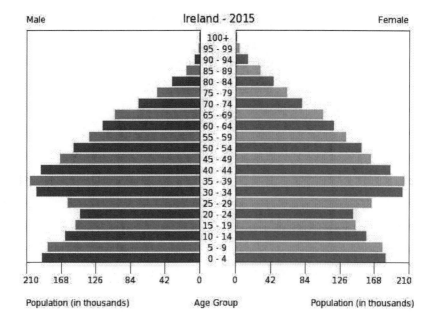

Very strong into 2026, Ireland will have a bust around that time but will slowly recover thereafter.

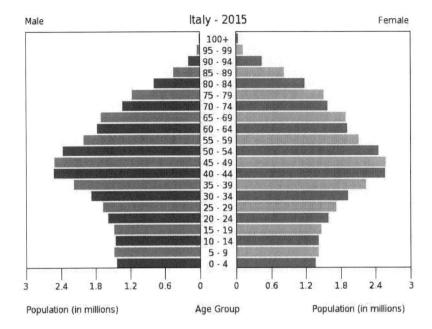

Italy will have a long-term weak curve in its economy.

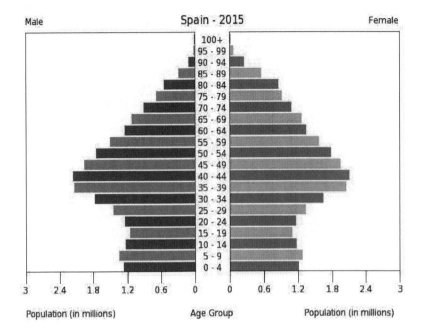

Spain will enter a rough patch in its economy in about 10 years.

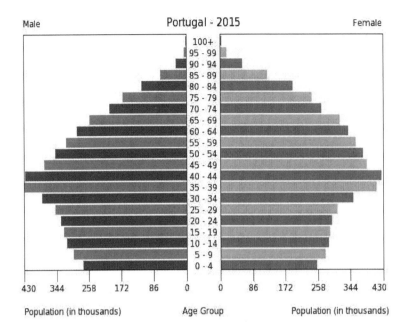

Portugal will do well for a small amount of time, but later on, its economy will weaken.

EASTERN EUROPE

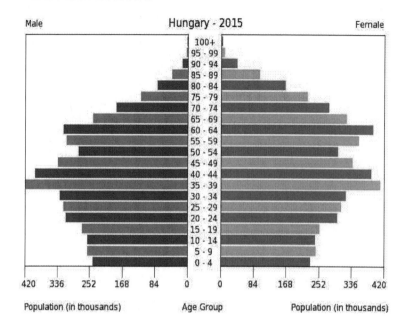

Hungary will stay strong for the next decade, but over time, it will enter a period of economic strife.

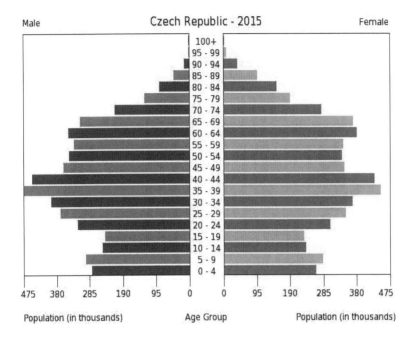

The Czech Republic will stay strong through the next decade, similarly to Hungary, and will slowly weaken afterward.

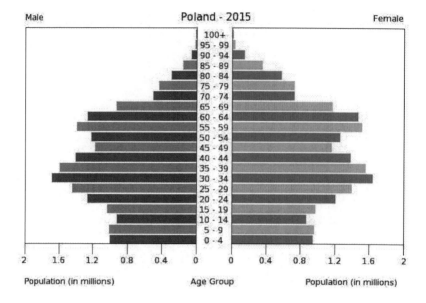

The Poles will have a very similar economy to Hungary and the Czech Republic, strong for the next decade with a later decrease in spending.

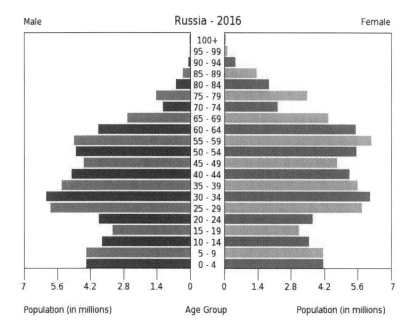

Once again, Russia will be strong for the next few years, but later on it will take a few hits.

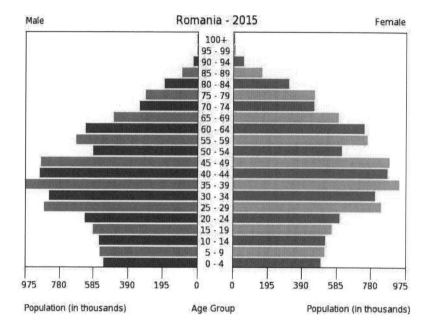

Romania will be strong for the next decade and weak afterward.

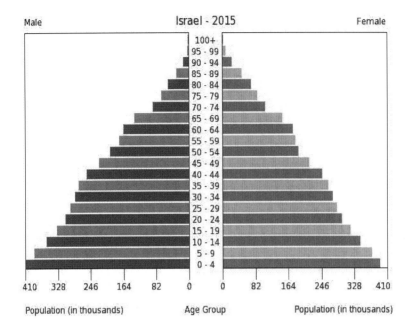

Israel's economy will flourish for the next 40 years, and there is no signs of it slowing down.

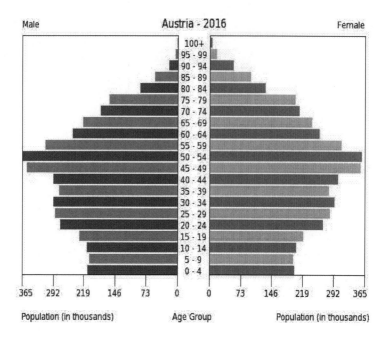

Austria is very bearish, especially compared to the rest of Eastern Europe.

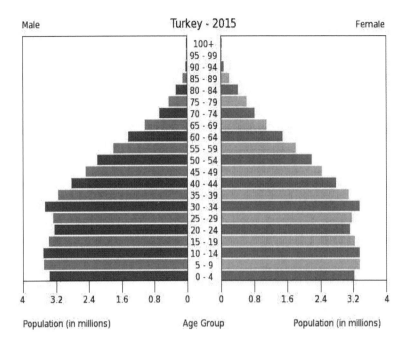

Turkey's economy is very strong, and will probably be one of the top economies in the coming decades.

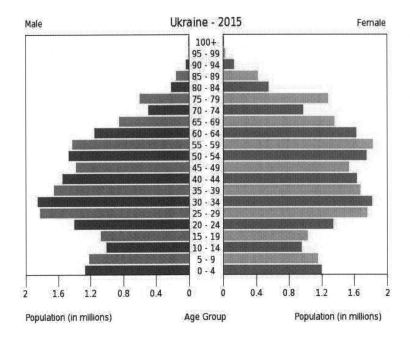

Ukraine has a very strong economy in the coming years, but will be bearish after around 20 years.

EAST ASIA

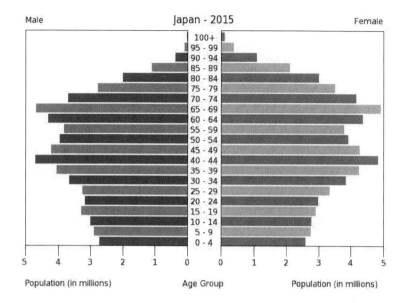

Japan's economy will have a nice rebound soon, but then will take a big hit and seriously weaken.

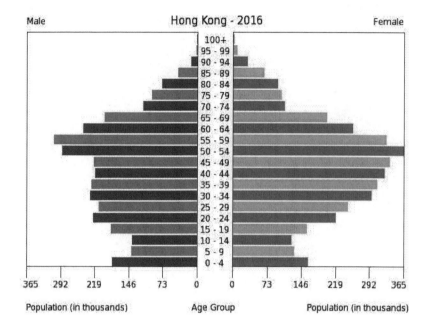

Because Hong Kong is a city-state, it is not of massive importance and is mainly here to compare to Japan as a developed east Asian nation. Hong Kong will be very bearish in the next few decades.

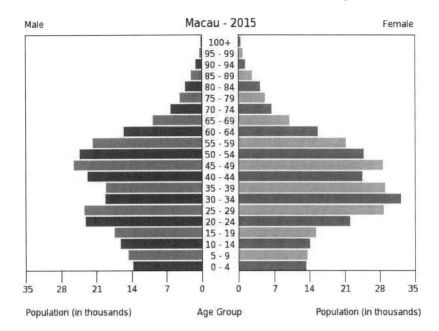

Macau is similar to Hong Kong, being a city-state, yet it will be strong for a little while in the future and ultimately weaken.

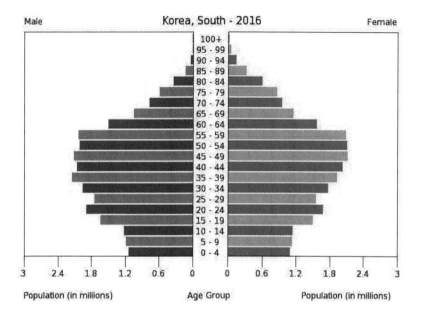

South Korea will be very weak in the future.

OCEANIA

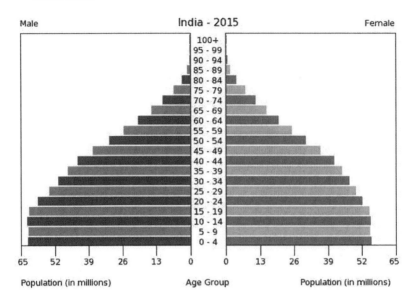

India will have a world-class economy and will most likely be the world's largest economy in the next four decades.

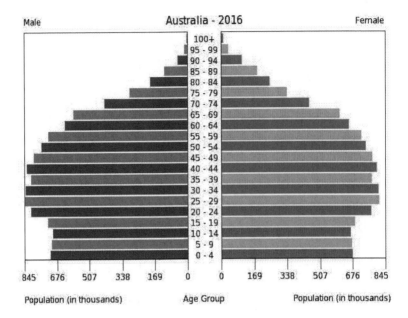

Australia will be another one of the world's top economies.

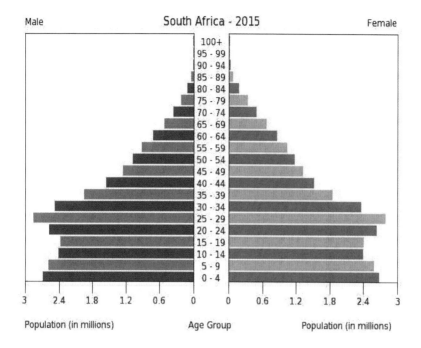

South Africa's economy will flourish soon enough, but will dip around 2046.

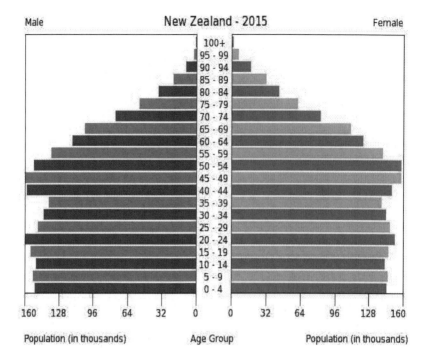

New Zealand will rise to a peak and plateau for the next 40 years.

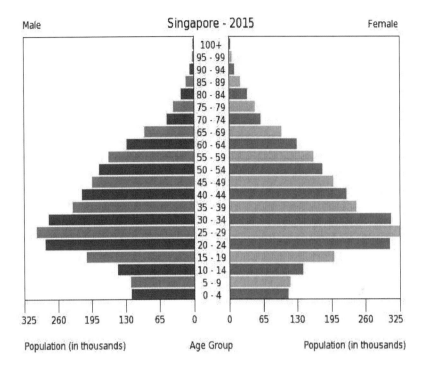

Singapore will do outstandingly well; however, in 2046 it will fall heavily.

In summation, these will be the top 10 economies in the next 50 years:

1. Mexico

2. Brazil

3. India

4. Australia

5. Canada

6. Turkey

7. South Africa

8. New Zealand

9. Israel

10. Haiti

Disclaimer:

It is important to remember, however, that these are forecasts and not guarantees—they are merely predictions about what is likely to become of the world's economies. Many unforeseen events may occur and change this list. Some countries that are not on this list may rise to the level of those on the list by adjusting their population age distribution by using immigration to fill in the gaps. These forecasts not guarantees.

In summary: The way to use this chapter is as a diversification tool by either investing internationally (especially in these top 10) or by changing your strategic/marketing plan by expanding into these top 10 economies, which are most likely to weather the next 15 years of economic doldrums.

CHAPTER 7

THE HISTORY OF TAXES

Understanding the history of taxes is vital in helping us spot legitimate threats caused by the aging of the population.

> "Those who cannot remember the past
> are condemned to repeat it"
>
> -George Santayana

THE CONSTITUTION

The US Constitution was written during the Philadelphia convention now known as the Constitutional convention, which was held from May 25 until the day the Constitution was signed on September 17, 1787.

Replacing the Articles of Confederation, the Constitution grants the federal government the power to tax the people, which freed the federal government from dependency on the states for tax revenue. The Constitution also enables the federal government to tax what it prefers as long as the tax is proportional to the populace. (This later becomes a challenge as the definition of "proportional" requires a constitutional amendment.)

The initial resistance to federal taxation manifested itself in the whiskey rebellion from 1791 to 1794, in which 500 armed men attacked the house of Gen. John Neville who was a tax inspector at the time. The suppression of the rebellion demonstrated that the new government had both the will and the ability to suppress violence in order to enforce its laws.

TARIFFS

A tariff is a tax placed on shipments of imported goods; by contrast, an excise tax is an indirect tax charged on the sale of one good.

Tadeusz Kosciuszko was a Polish military engineer who became a national hero in Poland, Lithuania, Belarus, and the United States. He helped design West Point, served the Continental Congress as brigadier general, and was a lifelong friend of Thomas Jefferson. To develop a historical context for our discussion of taxation, let us look at what Jefferson wrote to Kosciuszko:

The rich alone use imported articles, and on these alone the whole taxes of the general government are levied. The poor man who uses nothing but what is made in his own farm or family, or within his own country, he pays not a farthing of tax to the general government.

Up until the Civil War, tariffs constituted the overwhelming majority of all tax revenue for the federal government. The remainder came from the sale of land.

Income tax could not exist early in the history of the Western world because income did not exist prior to the Industrial Revolution. Thus, income tax a relatively new invention.

THE CIVIL WAR

The Civil War dramatically altered the landscape of taxation. Some would consider it the costliest war in American history in terms of both lives and money. According to tax historians, federal tax revenue at the time totaled $53.5 million, of which $49.61 million came directly from tariffs. Wars cost money, and the Civil War forced all sorts of new forms of taxes. By 1866, tax revenue had increased to approximately $535, million a tenfold increase than prior to the war.

The first form of income tax was created in 1861. As the war increased in cost, so did the taxation of income. When you consider roughly all the taxes were now enforced on only the Northern states, that tenfold increase in taxation was really more like twentyfold increase on the citizens of the United States, now made up of Northern states. By 1866, income tax constituted more than one-half of US tax revenue. We can draw from this is that the tolerance for income taxes by the general public increased as a result of the war's costliness.

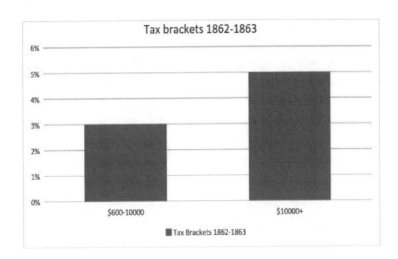

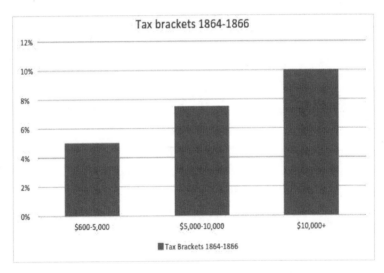

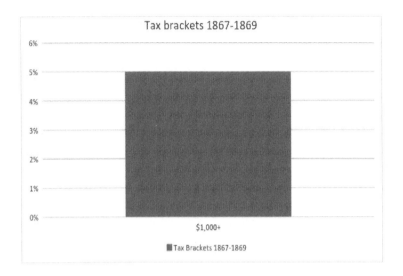

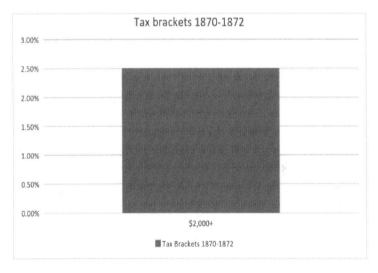

Income tax expired in 1872, and the federal government returned to its preferred method of taxation during the Reconstruction period following Lee's surrender at the Appomattox Courthouse.

Taxation by tariff burdens farmers more than manufacturers,

and there was a strong initiative in 1872 brought on by the Democratic Party to reenact an income tax to lessen that burden. This tax was struck down by the Supreme Court because it was deemed an unconstitutional direct tax. This ruling, although considered incorrect by legal scholars today, as a previous Supreme Court ruling deems such tax constitutional, put down any effort to tax income without changing the Constitution.

President William Howard Taft endorsed an amendment to the Constitution to permit the federal government to enact an income tax in 1909, but he failed. Woodrow Wilson, however, brought with him a Democratic majority to Congress, enabling the 16th amendment to be passed by both the House and Senate with surprising ease. Some historians believe this was due to the anticipation of entering World War I and the need for higher tax revenues.

WORLD WAR I

The so-called, "War to End all Wars" broke out on August 2, 1914, following the assassination of Archduke Franz Ferdinand. The 1913 tax act posed a 2 percent income tax on income in excess of $2,000 (approximately $46,200 in today's dollars). The highest tax rate at the time was 7 percent on income greater than $500,000 (or $21 million in today's dollars).

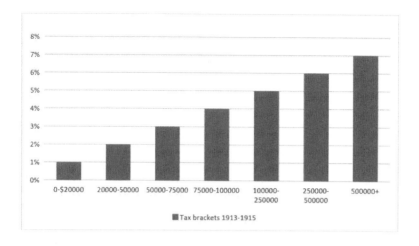

Few people paid a lot in income tax prior to World War I. That changed with formal entry into the war. The lowest tax rate jumped to 6 percent, while the highest increased more than tenfold, to 77 percent on income over $1 million ($42 million in today's dollars).

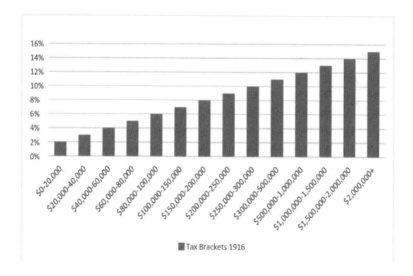

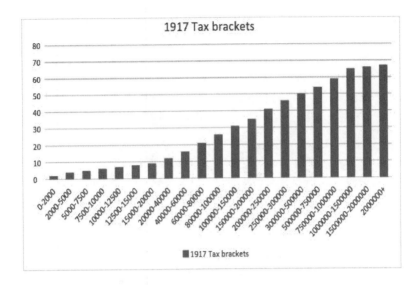

The federal government reduced postwar tax rates approximately four years after the end of World War I, although they were never to be as low as the pre-war tax rates.

THE ROARING 20S

Most fiscal policy of the 1920s was aimed at reducing taxes, which was successful for the most part. The combination of a roaring economy and an aggressive tax reduction policy caused tax brackets to fall overall.

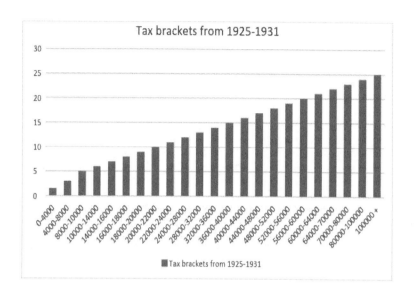

Tax brackets from 1925-1931

THE GREAT DEPRESSION

The Great Depression in the US started with the stock market crash on October 24, 1929, and lasted until the late 1930s. It is commonly thought of as the lowest any economy in the world could sink to. Industrial trade fell by 50 percent, and unemployment rose to 25 percent. This was obviously the worst of times, especially when you consider that most women were not part of the workforce. Personal income dropped, and, therefore, income tax revenue dropped, decimating federal finances. Tax receipts fell by 50 percent, while related government spending needed to roughly double. Tax rates were increased to reduce the deficit; the lowest levels increased from 1.5 percent to 4 percent, and the highest levels went from 25 percent to 63 percent. Excise taxes were increased significantly.

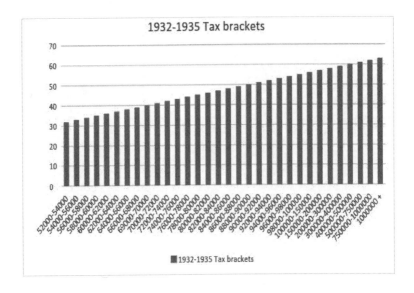

FDR IMPOSES TAXES ON THE RICH

President Franklin Delano Roosevelt entered office on March 4, 1933, and did little to affect taxation until 1935, at which time he raised taxes on the rich significantly. This was driven less by revenue and more by "fairness." FDR sent a letter to Congress:

People know that vast income comes not only by effort, ability, or luck, but by opportunity for advancement provided by the government. Therefore the burden to pay for the government should fall to those who benefit most.

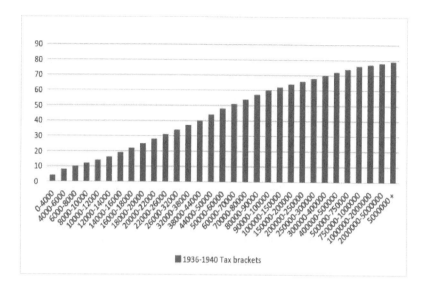

Roosevelt feared the growing socialist sentiment among the disenfranchised and saw organizations like the Communist Party as a threat. Therefore, he used taxation policy to appear hard on the rich in order to present the capitalist system as fairer. The 1935 tax bill raised the highest rate to 79 percent of people earning more than $5 million a year (approximately $80 million in today's dollars). It was rumored that only one person, oil tycoon John D. Rockefeller, was subject to the highest tax rate. Social Security was enacted that same year; some might say it was yet another form of taxation.

WORLD WAR II

Considered by most historians to be what pulled the US out of the Depression, World War II did little to help alleviate the high tax environment of the depression era, and ultimately led to the highest level of taxes ever seen in the history of the United States. In addition, it broadened the tax base from the rich to include the middle class. At the beginning of the war, less than 5 percent of all people paid income taxes. In 1939, only $4 million was filed in tax returns; by the end of the war, that number had increased tenfold.

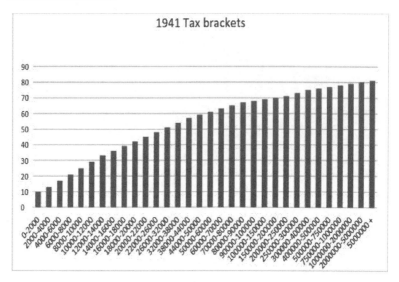

The lowest rates were raised from 4 percent to 13 percent of incomes greater than $2,000 (approximately $24,000 in today's dollars).

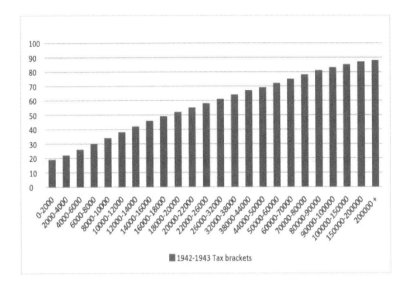

1942-1943 Tax brackets

The top rate increased to an unprecedented 94 percent of income higher than $200,000. The equivalent of $2.4 million per annum is the highest tax rate ever in the history of taxes in the United States. After the war, rates were reduced, but not by much. It seems the Depression era affected changes in taxation culture as Americans became, much like Europe, tolerant of high taxes.

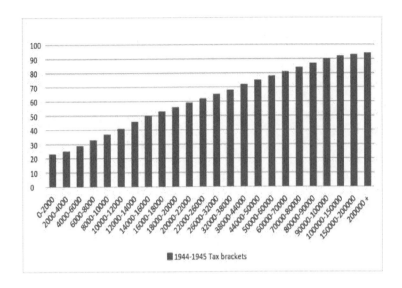

The Cold War and the Red Scare prevented taxes from being cut back much. Taxes were never returned to their pre-World War II lows.

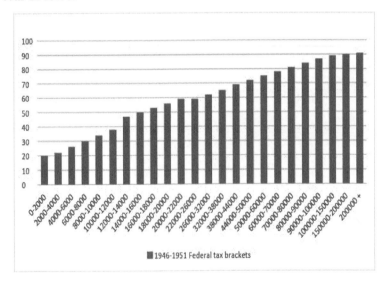

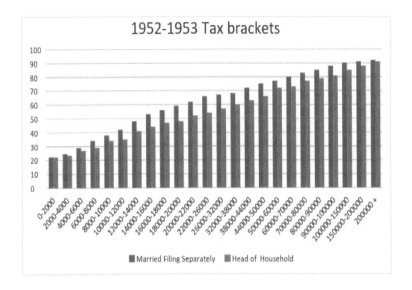

The strategy of using taxation as a moral guideline first appears in 1952, with the first appearance of taxation rules that favor remaining married. There is evidence throughout taxation history that the government influences morality through taxation as opposed to legislation. Forced morality isn't morality at all; for example, one can encourage moral deeds through taxation by giving tax breaks to those who are charitable.

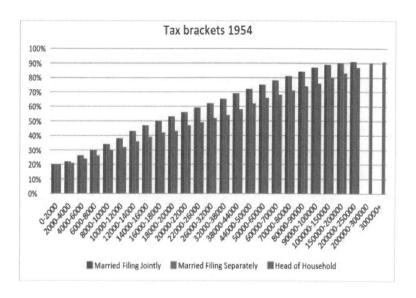

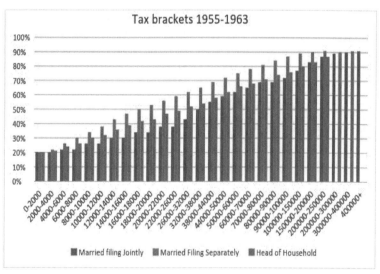

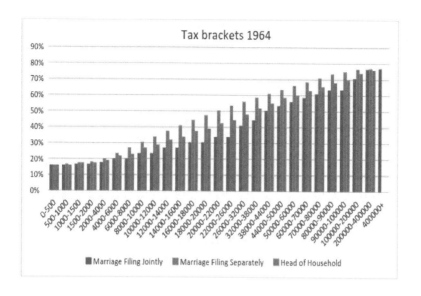

LBJ TAX CUT OF 1964

Although originally proposed by President John F. Kennedy, in 1964, Lyndon Baines Johnson had the lowest rate dropped from 20 percent to 14 percent and the highest rate to be reduced to 70 percent of income.

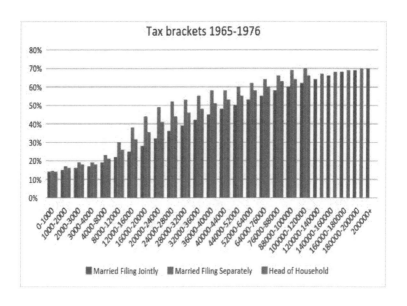

Tax brackets 1965-1976

■ Married Filing Jointly   ■ Married Filing Separately   ■ Head of Household

REAGAN-ERA TAX CUTS

President Ronald Reagan ran on a platform promising to replicate the tax changes of the Kennedy era, affecting broad tax cuts, in effect, ushering in Reaganomics and the trickle-down theory of taxation—and effectively changing the culture of high taxation tolerance by the American citizen. Personally, I believe the combination of the US economy transitioning from a manufacturing to a service-based economy had a great deal to do with this.

If my salary is fixed, then I know what my tax bracket will be next year. I will likely vote for the candidate that favors taxing *me* less.

Rich is a relative term. I have presented to audiences where the average net worth was $52 million, and none of them consider themselves rich.

As we switch to a service-based economy, the ceiling on income changes. People working in a service-based economy believe that they can one day be rich because they no longer have a limited income and will therefore be less tolerant of taxes on the rich. As a result, they can be easily manipulated by conservative politicians to vote for lower taxes on higher tax brackets. These politicians are higher in tax brackets themselves and are, in truth, looking for lower taxes on themselves and not looking out for the little guy.

If my salary has no limit, I might rise to a very high tax bracket next year. I will likely vote for the candidate who taxes rich people less.

The 1980 tax cut brought the highest rates down to 50 percent and the bottom rate from 14 percent to 9 percent.

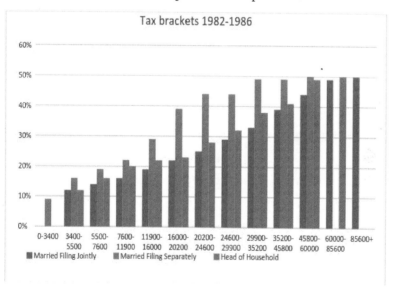

The 1986 Tax Reform Act raised the bottom rate from 11 percent to 15 percent and lowered the top rate from 50 percent to 28 percent. So on Reagan's watch, we in effect dropped the highest rate from the 70s down to 28 percent.

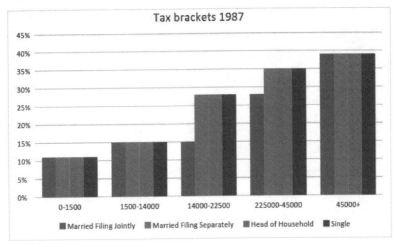

According to the architect of the last tax reform in this country's history, Bruce Bartlett, author of *The Benefit and the Burden: Tax Reform—Why We Need It and What It Will Take*, George H.W. Bush agreed to a budget deal raising the top rate from 28 percent to 31 percent, which evidently cost him reelection and poisoned the well for all future tax reform. One last note on income: it's a relatively new development. Throughout history, the majority of humanity had little or no income, so taxes were mainly levied on trade, and because there were few ports, trade was easy to measure. Property taxes were another easy-to-measure method of increasing revenue. The English Tudor is a type of architecture marked by its small windows. It can be said that is because at the time, the tax assessor could easily see how many windows you had and assess your taxes accordingly. It was easy to assume that if you had a lot of windows, you were rich, as windows were incredibly expensive to make. It was not until the

19th century that income was taxed. One could argue that prior to the Industrial Revolution, income did not exist for the large percentage of the populace.

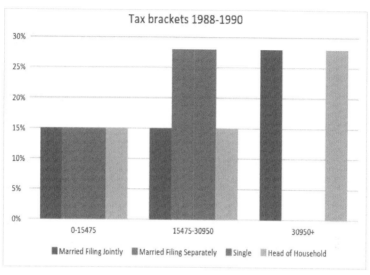

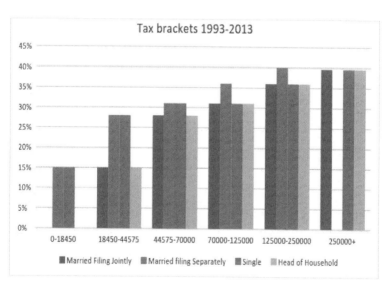

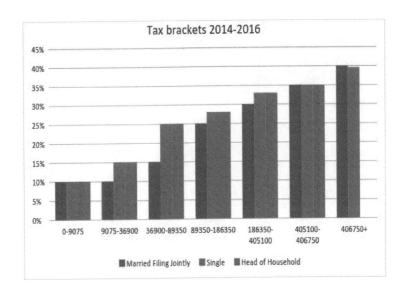

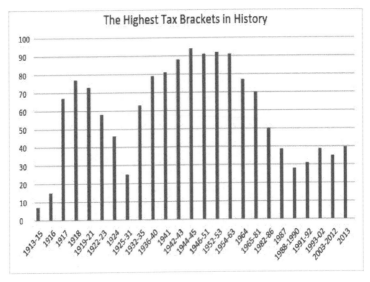

TAXATION PHILOSOPHY

Voters and media audiences tend to have short attention spans, responding mainly to sound bites, which in most cases leads to effective forms of communication. In the case of taxation, however, simplified sound bites, such as "high taxes = no growth," do not tell the whole story, and lead to serious misconceptions. Another factor clouding the truth is when you change a variable that affects the entirety of a system, you can never be certain it had the desired effect or was not the cause of the change. In addition, any scientist will tell you that the first law of research is that humans are guilty of seeing what they prefer to see.

For example, conservatives tend to see optimal levels of taxation as "zero," as if all taxation is legal thievery. If that were true, then no level of taxation can bedeemed moral.

When analyzing taxation, we cannot escape our political biases, and political biases are driven in large part by fear. For example, if I fear the greed of big business, then I am most likely to be a Democrat. If I fear big government and its inherent inefficiencies, then I am most likely to be Republican. Psychologists have long known that we will do more to avoid pain than we will to gain pleasure. So, as a result, fear is a great motivator and can be easily manipulated by a candidate to serve that candidate's agenda.

I confess to you that I am relatively agnostic about politics. This may be due to studying the subject for so long. I tend to view politicians the way an anthropologist would view a species. This gives me a unique perspective, where my fears and my emotions cannot be used to meet the politician's ends. It affords me the position of looking at politics from an "it is what it is" perspective. So I respectfully propose to you, the reader, to position yourself as neutrally as possible in order to gain as much value as you can from these pages. In return, I promise to not use your political views to manipulate you in any way.

Confirmation bias: The tendency to view new evidence as confirmation of one's theories or beliefs, despite that evidence sometimes being entirely false, misconstrued, or constructed information to suit someone's (probably a politician's) agenda.

ECONOMIC BOOM AND BUST PERIODS ARE UNDOUBTEDLY LINKED TO TAXATION

Understand there are boom and bust periods in the economy, and the typical short recession, although annoying, it is unlikely to derail your financial dreams. It is the downward cycle once every 20 years that could derail those dreams. These are the bust periods to worry about.

Typically financial advisors analyze a negative financial event from the long-term consequences perspective, and if the results of their analysis mean the threats for long-term financial consequences are minor, no changes to strategies will be recommended. Once every 10 or 20 years, there is a generational bad market where typically defensive strategies will be recommended by the advisor in order to avoid significant losses from what is referred to as "fundamental shifts in the economy," for example, the financial crisis of 2008-2009 or even the dot-com bubble bursting in the early 2000s.

At the start of a downward trend, how does one know if it is going to lead to a significant recession or if it will be short lived? It is the big ones that have a profound effect on the financial dreams and aspirations of investors, especially if you just retired at the start of one.

One could even argue almost all causes for economic downturns are unpredictable, but understanding shifts in demographics give us the power to predict spending trends potentially decades in advance. This has the ability to predict positive and negative swings for any industry.

Caveat: Spending patterns are not the be all and end all of economics swings.

Unfortunately, there are a good many variables outside of our control, but at the very least, we have predictable spending patterns and demographics, and they are by far the most influential of all the variables.

WHY DOES THE GOVERNMENT EXIST?

Most people have misconceptions about why the government exists. I am fairly certain the government does not exist to make a profit for you or themselves. In my experience, if you ask the question of any audience, you will elicit numerous responses, most of which are unflattering.

I propose that the government exists for one purpose: *to create stability*.

When Washington and the founding fathers set out to create a more perfect union, one thing was clear: we needed a strong central government. The dependence of the early federal government on tax revenue handouts from the states crippled Washington's army, and any statesmen at the time knew the English would one day return. And they actually did, in the War of 1812. Washington understood we needed to centralize power in the federal government, specifically the power to tax in order to pay for the defense of our sovereignty and our coveted vast supply of natural resources. Central power in the federal government is a democratic view today, and one could argue that Washington was our first Democrat. He feared the English military might, so much so that he invented our first centralized government, as it would provide the stability we lacked in the Revolutionary War.

In the early 2000s, I was asked to present to a trade association for the heads of security for many of the buildings in Manhattan, and the topic of unemployment came up in our conversation. I asked the question "Who's more dangerous, a high school dropout with a handgun or pissed-off engineer?"

This question underscores the question of stability that governments provide. Unemployment, depending on its severity, can undermine stability. One could argue that the very high level of unemployment that existed during the Great Depression could have completely undermined the American government and caused either nonviolent or violent revolution.

The security industry, as a whole, is populated by ex-CIA, ex-military, and ex-police, so it should come as no surprise when people trained most of their adult life on the subject of security/safety—once they retire from government work—continue the career in the private sector. It was determined by the audience of this trade association that a disenfranchised engineer can kill more people than a high school dropout with a handgun because he understands the weaknesses of large structures and the physics behind destroying them. Therefore, the engineer was deemed more dangerous.

This underlies the theme that politicians understand that high levels of unemployment are dangerous for society, and FDR understood this better than most. When he raised the highest tax level of income tax to 79 percent in 1935, this action was not about tax revenue, because it did not produce much. It was about appearing fair. Creating the New Deal and programs like the Civilian Conservation Corps (CCC) and the Works Progress Administration (WPA) were actions to employ the nation. In other words, if the private sector cannot employ the nation profitably, then it becomes the government's obligation to do so. The government has no duty to produce profit, just a sacred duty to produce stability.

I have developed a philosophy in my presentations: "If I say something clever, you're welcome to steal it; if you say something clever, I'm going to steal it." I was presenting in Eau Claire, Wisconsin, and when I got to the subject of taxes, there was one CEO who was smiling the entire time. This portion of my presentation tends to elicit anger, victim mentality, and even some minor violence, and no one prior to or since has ever smiled, I felt the need to stop and check in with him. Was he high? Deranged? Or what? His response was fascinating:

He simply stated, "Oh, I view taxes as revolution insurance."

I propose to you to steal this philosophy as I have, and if you do so, no politician or advisor can move your emotions to suit their needs. This is an example of what Bruce Bartlett, author of the bestseller *The Benefit and the Burden*, means by "the benefit."

ARE YOU RICH?

In my presentations, I ask this question regularly, so much so that the cumulative answers border on empirical research. One of my first presentations was to a peer advisory group that was on retreat in Chicago. A peer advisory group is an ad hoc board of directors of non-publicly traded CEOs who do not compete with each other and have no financial connection to each other.

The average net worth of this particular group turned out to be $52 million each. Yet when I asked the question, "Are you rich? Who here considers himself rich?, no hands went in the air. So how is it that people who would easily be considered rich by nearly every other human being do not consider themselves rich?

It turns out that rich is a relative term, meaning anyone with at least a dollar more than me.

It also seems that the term "wealthy" is relative, and its definition seems to be just as elusive as rich. In a related study, I asked the respondents to answer yes or no to the question, "Are you wealthy?" The results were quite surprising: all respondents with a net worth of less than $1.5 million answered yes to the question, whereas all respondents worth more than $1.5 million said no. My work in finance and interviews with clients of all echelons of net worth have led me to believe that there is a correlation between becoming wealthy and being paranoid about being poor.

There seems to be a vast difference between our own definition of rich and the government's definition of rich. When asked, "What's the government's definition of rich?" most people respond, "$200,000 or more in annual income." This is by far the most common response.

"Let me get this straight. If I lie to the government, it's a felony. If the government lies to me, it's politics"—attributed to Bill Murray

At the time of this writing, the average yearly income of the average American is approximately $52,000 combined (husband and wife). I would imagine if you're sharp enough to pick up a book like this, your income is significantly higher than that. I would view this as a threat, as one could argue if the average combined income in America is $52,000 a year, the government's definition of rich is "a dollar more a dollar richer." The country has a long history of taxing more when it needs it, as discussed above. I humbly submit to you that if the government did not need more revenue, red traffic light cameras would not exist.

WE OWE A DEBT TO TALKING HEAD CONSERVATIVES.

Conservatives sometimes hurt their own cause, for example, a union member voting for Donald Trump for president. Actor Carroll O'Connor portrayed Archie Bunker, an ultra-conservative union dockworker on the popular television show "All in the Family." For all intents and purposes, union workers like Archie had a ceiling on what they could make. And talking head conservatives can exploit these voters' emotions by convincing them that it is not in anyone's best interests to have estate taxes. Whereas in Archie's case, he would not have been affected by estate taxes, as he made too little to qualify. Political conservatives and taxation conservatives do not need to go hand in hand, and, in some cases, especially in the poor and middle class, political conservatives actually hurt their own case by being a taxation conservative. And it is the talking head conservative that likely benefited the most.

Judging from the advertising on satellite radio, we can assume that long-haul truckers are a key demographic for long-form talk radio. My belief is that talking head conservatives convinced their audience, long-haul truckers and other political conservatives of the lower middle-class, that we should never have estate taxes, for any number of reasons, but "because they [long-haul truckers] might have an estate tax problem" seems to be a relatively new theme.

Once long-haul truckers figure out they are never going to have estate tax problem, no matter what, then everyone reading these pages will suddenly have an estate tax problem—unless the long-haul trucker owns the company, which is improbable or at least it's improbable that they'd be listening to long-form talk radio. Long-haul truckers won't ever have an estate tax problem, but conservatives want them thinking that they will. And this is just one of many ways that talking heads can get people to vote against their own best interests.

SOCIALISM VERSUS CAPITALISM

What is the difference between socialism and capitalism?

I propose that there are no true Communist or Capitalist states in the world. If you use the example of the U.S.S.R. as a dictatorship—where tolerance hardly ever showed its face and mercy for the accused was unheard of—and compare it to a case of "true" capitalism, Bogotá, Columbia, in 1980 comes to mind. There you would have to send your kids to a school that you built and paid for, taught by teachers on your payroll, and escort them with the security force living off your money. Every developed nation is ultimately a shade of gray of socialism in between true capitalism and true communism

The difference between socialism and capitalism comes down to taxation policy.

We need to embrace the fact that we have lived in a variable socialist state since the advent of income taxes. Once you realize the validity of this statement, you can see that we have lived through a socialist style of taxation for most of the 20th century, and during that time, we accomplished some remarkable feats. For example, the Hoover dam, landing on the moon, workforce projects, and even the highway bill were great work projects under a socialist style of taxation, and many of these are starting to fall into disrepair since we abandoned this style of taxation in favor of a more capitalist form of taxation. There are always consequences for tax reform some good, some bad—it all depends on your perspective of good and bad taxation policy.

THE TAX SEESAW

The aging of the baby boom generation and its subsequent changes in spending habits will have a profound effect on both the collection of tax revenue and the demand for entitlement programs, such as Medicare and Social Security (contributory) and Medicaid (non-contributory). If we look at tax as a seesaw, we can see when and where the future threats lie. In order to glean the most value from this next exercise, we have to assume we are at what is referred to as tax equilibrium, which means that we are bringing in as much tax revenue as we are paying out. I know we are not, but please play my reindeer games, and you will gain more from this next exercise and enable yourself to prepare for whatever threats lie ahead.

Tax Demand   Tax Revenue

If we are declining in the number of people at the magic age of 49½ and, even more importantly, declining in the number of people at the magic age of 55 during the next decade and a half, one can assume consumer spending will naturally dry up as people age and we transition to the smaller generation X. Generation X cannot make up for the difference in spending.

If consumer spending dries up, what will happen to sales tax revenue over the next decade and a half? The overwhelming response in my surveys is that sales tax revenue will decline as a result of empty-nest spending syndrome for the baby boom generation, resulting in a change in spending patterns and the inability for generation X to make up the difference in spending due to its smaller size.

Tax Demand   Tax Revenue

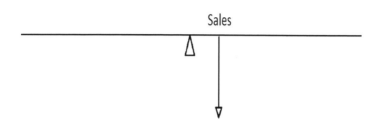

In addition, we are tripling the number of 65-year-olds over the next half a decade so I submit to you: "When people are retired, do they pay less in taxes than before they retired?" The overwhelming response from my audiences is yes, they pay less in taxes, which will have profound effect on tax revenue receipts.

Tax Demand   Tax Revenue

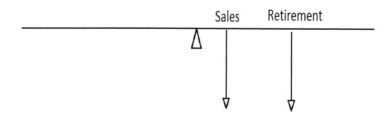

As consumer spending dries up naturally over the next decade and a half as the baby boom generation transitions to the empty-nest stage of life, we can expect higher unemployment. Retail sales are two-thirds of the economy, and if consumer spending is decreasing, that will have a direct, negative impact on retail sales, ultimately causing higher employment. So in order to analyze the effect on tax revenue, all you has to do is ask yourself, "Do people pay more in taxes when they're unemployed than when they were working?" Although the answer appears obvious, it is important to make sure we are on the same page. Under-employment, which is the result of age wave spending patterns, illustrates how the age wave spending patterns cause boom periods and bust periods in the economy. Those taxes that are sensitive to spending pattern changes will be negatively affected as we transition from this peak spending age of the baby boom generation.

Tax Demand   Tax Revenue

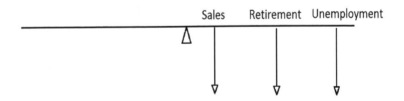

Sales   Retirement   Unemployment

Now let's look at the tax demand side of this exercise. If we are tripling the number of 65-year-olds in the next half decade, we have to assume that the demand for entitlement programs such as Social Security will increase dramatically.

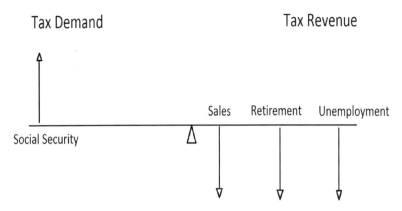

Similar to Social Security, the demand for the entitlement program Medicare will increase dramatically.

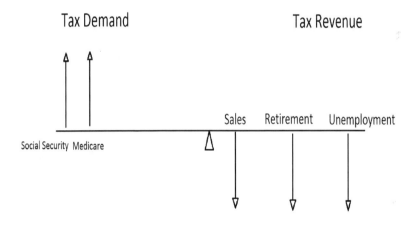

We have already discussed unemployment increasing as a result of the change in spending patterns when baby boomers reach their empty nest days. When we examine the economic effects of this dynamic from a tax demand perspective, we have to assume that the demand for unemployment benefits will increase.

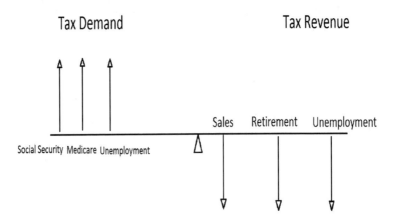

The dynamics that affect unemployment also will likely increase the demand for publicly funded welfare programs.

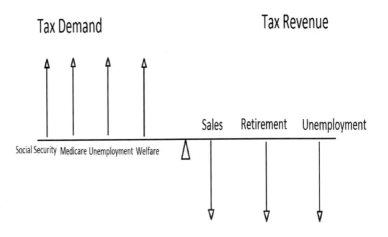

When you consider that the majority of all industrialized countries echo the same demographic patterns as the United States—their baby boom generation came just prior to and after

World War II—and the spending pattern of human beings are virtually the same regardless of the country they are living in. Therefore, the economic cycles of most of the world's industrialized nations should also echo the United States as their spending patterns follow that of their population and its age distribution.

What we are really talking about is worldwide financial doldrums brought on by the maturation of the majority of all industrialized economies.

As consumer spending decreases naturally across the globe, this will likely bring on worldwide financial troubles. Ask yourself: does this dynamic increase the likelihood of war?

When two under-industrialized countries are living next to each other and living in a state of financial lack, does this increase the likelihood of conflict? According to my audiences, the answer is an overwhelming yes. Therefore, we would likely have to increase the budget for defense as a result of new socioeconomic threats brought on by financial lack in under-industrialized countries.

In a recent presentation, I saw the former deputy director of the CIA under Reagan, Herb Meyer, who talked about how democracies do not tend to go to war unless for intervention purposes and how the middle-class does not like war, so it is not the industrialized nations we need to worry about. But a threat is a threat, and the likelihood is that we will have to increase the budget for defense for these new threats. My belief is that scarcity breeds conflict, and as the major economic powerhouses start their years of financial doldrums, the rest of the world will be negatively affected.

WHEN THE US SNEEZES, THE WORLD CATCHES A COLD.

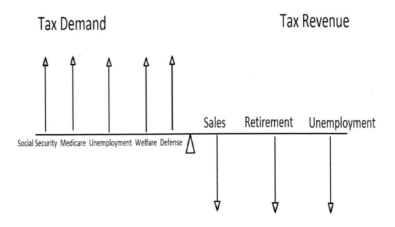

Lastly, we would have to repay all the drunken-sailor spending we have done over the past decade. When I said this at a presentation, it elicited a hilarious response from a Florida CEO. He instantly sat up and declared, "That's an insult to drunken sailors" and produced an op-ed piece he had written to the local paper. As a former "drunken sailor," in it he declared that he only ever spent his own money. This produced an enormous amount of laughter in the room.

The only way to pay for major expenses like bailouts, stimulus packages, or expensive wars is through taxes.

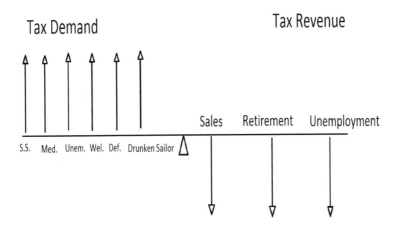

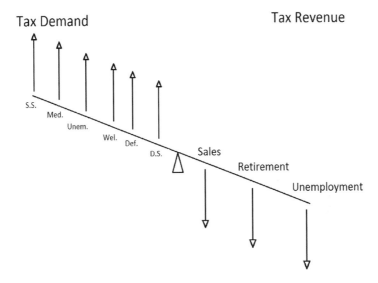

All of this points to significant tax increases in the future.

Eighty percent of my audiences are Republican, and if we take New York and California out of the equation, the percentage of Republicans in my audiences climb to more like 99.99 percent.

The classic Republican argument against tax increases is referred to as the Ayn Rand argument, from her book *Atlas Shrugged,* published in 1957. Keep in mind the '50s were marked by the highest level of taxation in US history.

The Republican Party is sometimes referred to as the grand old party, or GOP for short, and the classic GOP block to raising taxes is ...

"If you raise my taxes, that's a disincentive for me to work hard."

In other words, the **rich will go on strike** if the government raises taxes. I believe this to be a falsehood. Through my observational research and my surveys (of both my clients and my Vistage audiences) I know the CEOs of private, middle-market companies are some of the hardest-working people in the world.

Average working hours per week for CEOs in my survey

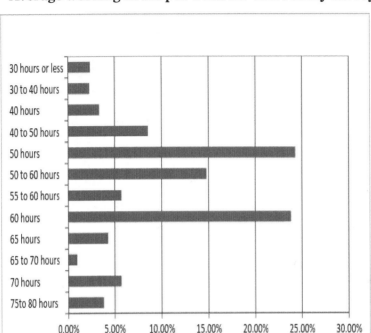

Based on my surveys, the average work week of private CEOs consists of 55 hours a week, with as reported low of 35 hours and a high of 80 hours a week. By anyone's standards, these are incredibly industrious people, so industrious that even they believe **if the government raises their taxes, they will simply work** harder. I believe the Ayn Rand argument fails partially because of how industrious these particular people are and also because most people believe they are paying too much in taxes currently, not realizing we are living with some of the lowest taxes in income tax history. The goal of taxation philosophy is to find the ideal level of tax where the government maximizes tax revenue yet does not incentivize taxpayers to spend all their time looking for tax loopholes.

WHAT'S JOB NUMBER ONE?

What most fail to realize is that political office is a career for most politicians, and they need to stay in office to earn a living, so job number one is to get reelected. The president and Congress need to fix the United States' challenges while pissing off the fewest number of voters. Although this may not sound morally correct or politically correct (given the pop culture definition of the day), it is a correct battle strategy for the newly elected president. Once we have established this as the lens we see political thought through, we can clearly spot threats to our businesses and our net worth.

WHO ARE THE EASIEST PEOPLE IN THE WORLD TO TAX?

Dead people.

THE HISTORY OF ESTATE TAXES

Estate taxes are an excise tax on the transfer of wealth the time of death.

Inheritance taxes are an excise tax on the receipt of property from the decedent.

Tax on property at the time of death dates back to ancient Egypt 700 B.C.E. and is likely even older than 2000 B.C.E. Augustus Caesar imposed a tax on legacy, on the subjects of Roman rule. There are also countless examples of death taxes throughout medieval Europe. By the 18th century, taxes imposed on documents and inventory of inheritance were adopted by most countries. Even the early United States experimented and with a "stamp tax," as it was known. This revenue stream was used to pay for the creation of the US Navy, which was needed due to European threats. In the early history of the United States, we were in an unofficial war with France and some of the other European states for our natural resources.

THE STAMP ACT OF 1797

Federal stamps were required on documents such wills and inherited inventory. This tax was repealed with the cessation of hostilities in 1802.

THE REVENUE ACT OF 1862

As stated earlier, the demand for revenue in the run-up to the Civil War created an environment of tax tolerance and need for innovative taxes. The revenue act of 1862 enabled the federal government seek new sources of revenue in the form of inheritance tax/death taxes. By 1864, the cost of the Civil War grew twentyfold, and modifications to the Revenue Act were enacted to include tax on bequests of real estate. By 1872, all these taxes were repealed.

SPANISH AMERICAN WAR AND THE WAR REVENUE ACT OF 1898

Once again, an expensive war caused a resurgence in estate taxes. This tax was repealed after the war in 1902.

THE 16TH AMENDMENT

This amendment to the Constitution paved the way for the modern era of estate taxes. The revenue act of 1916 created estate taxes in the modern sense. This tax was levied on the estate as opposed to a direct tax on beneficiaries.

Estate taxes have existed in varying forms for 90-plus years, with significant changes coming in the years 1948, 1976, and 2001.

The economic growth and tax relief reconciliation act of 2001 provided the eventual repeal of estate taxes for the majority of most people. Estates worth more than $5,450,000 would still pay estate taxes as of 2016.

In conclusion, if history is any indication, estate taxes tend to return when the government needs tax revenue, typically to pay for expensive wars. It would be naïve to think estate taxes are to stay in their current state, and I would plan for their return, as the government will need money in the coming decade.

DRIVING WHILE LOOKING THROUGH THE REARVIEW MIRROR

Most advisors lack strategic sight as they metaphorically throw their hands in the air, believing their world is governed by the current political environment. Most advisors—legal, financial, or otherwise—are metaphorically standing at the back of our boat looking at the wake and telling us what we should or shouldn't have done, and of course it's too late to undo these actions. What we need are advisors who have moved from the back of the boat into the pilot and help us look forward as we proceed into the future. My belief is that the majority of advisors are governed by the current political environment, and this creates an army of well-meaning professionals who lack foresight and the ability to truly advise us.

Income taxes are a relatively new invention, as income did not exist until the Industrial Revolution. The main taxes throughout history were trade tariffs and property tax. Taxes even shaped architectural and furniture design throughout history. An English Tudor, one of my favorite types of homes in this architectural movement, was partially created by taxes. At the time the Tudor movement started, property taxes were assessed by the size and the number of windows you had. Because windows, a relatively new invention at the time were expensive, it was assumed that a person with a lot of windows was rich and thus could afford higher taxes. So, therefore, smaller windows and fewer windows are what make up one of the distinctive characteristics of an English Tudor home.

Have you ever wondered why armoire is a French word? At the time of its invention, people were taxed on the size and the amount of their closet space, so the French invented a type of furniture that could function as a closet, yet not provoke the property taxes.

Looking to the past can sometimes help us understand where the threats lie in our future. As the population ages the burden of taxation falls of the next generation and puts significant pressure on raising taxes.

CHAPTER 8

ALL THE INDUSTRIES THAT WILL THRIVE IN THE NEXT 15 YEARS AND WHY IT'S SO IMPORTANT TO KNOW THEM

This chapter outlines the various industries that will not be negatively affected by recession and/or will benefit from the aging of the population. The author, having performed the exercise described below with more than 7,000 CEOs and C-level executives of the private middle markets, outlines their best suggestions for investment, employment, and start-up businesses. The reader will now know whether his or her future is in jeopardy or not.

WHAT TO DO WITH THIS INFORMATION

"If you want to get rich concentrate your assets. If you want to stay rich, diversify your assets." — Unknown

I run an exercise where CEOs and/or C-level executives pair off and each group is tasked with presenting as many examples as they can of classically recession-resistant businesses and businesses that will benefit from the aging of the population. For example, if you manufacture grab bars (a safety device to hold on to designed to enable a person to maintain their balance, lessen fatigue, or decrease the chance of a fall), I am not worried about your prospects. As baby boomers enter their golden years, the demand for grab bars will increase exponentially.

I have run this experiment with approximately 3,500 companies, so their responses border on statistically relevant.

The answers are as follows:

HEALTHCARE

Which can be broken out into numerous categories such as:

Pharmaceuticals

Nursing Homes

Home Healthcare

Hospitals

Assisted Living Facilities

Medical Imaging

Hospice Care

Medical Devices

Government Work. In every election cycle, the US economy goes in the dumps in the second or third year. The president has to look like he is doing something, and so comes up with an initiative or "stimulus plan," such as improving infrastructure, expanding the military, and Obama's "green plan."

In the wake of the subprime mortgage crisis (now known as the financial crisis), the Economic Stimulus and Reinvestment Act of 2009, was passed in a desperate attempt to ameliorate economic conditions. Its purpose was to create jobs immediately, including direct spending on infrastructure, education, health, and energy. Each of these areas benefitted from this move to counter the Great Recession.

These actions come out of Keynesian macroeconomic theory, which argues that during recessions, the government has to take up the mantle of spending in order to stop the economic deterioration.

Discount Store. Spending money can make one euphoric, and one could argue that if I cannot afford Nordstrom in a recession, I can get that same high from a discount store. According to a study from the *Journal of Consumer Psychology*, we enjoy spending money because it allows us a sense of control, and during a recession/ depression there is not a large sense of control.

Law. Litigation, bankruptcy, elder, estate

These will likely thrive as a result of the aging of the population and the probable economic slowdown as consumer spending trails off naturally. Tough economic times create conflict between partners (whether marriage or business), and as people get poorer, they become more likely to sue. As a result litigation flourishes as an industry. As the baby boomers age, they spend less and less, increasing unemployment due to unsuccessful businesses and thus bankruptcy. Elder law will grow in profits as the population ages due to the needs of the elderly and the legality of their care and protection. If a law firm does not have an expert in elder law, it had better get one—or several. Estate law, for those who don't already know, has to do with the inheritance from a recently deceased person to his or her successors; this category of law will also do very well for obvious reasons.

Insurance. Insurance is classically recession resistant for two reasons: first, certain insurance is mandatory by regulation (e.g., car insurance and liability insurance for businesses), and, second, it can be the last bastion for tax income advantages and certain tax benefits.

Life insurance for death benefit, although not required by law, is extremely prevalent. It is estimated that 80 percent of all voters own some type of life insurance, which explains why it is such an uphill political battle to take away its tax preferences. Each president who has attempted to take away the tax benefit of life insurance was met with failure. My belief is that it affects too many people and therefore pisses off too many voters.

Tax status vulnerability of investment vehicles:

Roth IRA	
Pros	Cons
Free of any tax penalties	Tax bracket could change
Many different investment possibilities	Income limitations
No age limit	Contribution limits
Inexpensive	The government can change the tax status after the fact
Municipal Bonds	
Pros	Cons
Free of Tax Penalties	Less likely to beat inflation
Likely not as risky as the stock market	Risk of income rates changing
Very high liquidity	Risk of default*
Due to tax benefits it will compound	Not profitable for people in a low tax bracket

Life Insurance (as an investment) AKA Roth IRA Alternative	
Pros	Cons
Potential returns	Mediocre Returns
Fixed Expenses	Large Expenses
Able to be withdrawn before death	Very complicated and difficult to understand
Potential tax free income as loans	
Most voters own Life Insurance, which minimizes susceptibility to political threats	

Maintenance. When times are tough, people tend to keep their things longer and the sale of new items plummets as the maintenance demands for old items skyrockets. In the world of mergers and acquisitions, maintenance contracts are able to prove the sustainability and durability of the business, significantly impacting the valuation of the business at the time of sale.

Think of all the baby boomers who will prefer to live in their current home. These houses will need to be converted to safe houses for the elderly, and those same homes will be needed to be maintained as the home owner loses their capacity to care for it.

From a commercial perspective: I was presenting in California to what turned out to be the largest cement producer in the state of California, an economic powerhouse before the recession. After the financial crisis, the company had fallen into decline due to the crisis. When the credit markets are seized, which is exactly what happened in 2008 and after, nothing sold through financing (e.g., cars, appliances, homes, new construction) can be purchased and the contracts for new construction dry up.

The CEO realized his mistake. Being dependent on new construction as his only source of revenue was great when things were booming, until they weren't. He reminded his C-levels they had acquired a building materials company prior to the Great Recession, but had abandoned it in an attempt to save the goose that laid his golden egg. Because the cement company was much larger, it seemed the correct thing to do, and maybe it was. But now that the economy has improved, it was important to focus on the building materials company as a non-correlated business. Building materials are used in rehabilitating old structures and are therefore not as dependent on financing, providing the overall organization another income stream.

Healthcare. Medical devices, pharmaceuticals, chemicals, biotechnology companies, and companies that manage clinics and hospitals.

Agriculture. Supermarkets, farming machine and supply companies, agribusiness, agrichemical suppliers and producers, crop-breeding companies, farming and contract farming, seed supply and processing. Remember, you need a farmer 3 times a day.

Death. Crematoriums, funeral homes, coffin/casket suppliers, headstone and memorial craftsmen, morgues, cemetery plots.

Religion. Holy book producers; manufacturers of holy symbols, food, drinks, etc.; church/mosque/monastery/temple architects and builders; religious organizations.

Energy. Green energy research and development; resource location, gathering, and refinement; and energy transportation and storage.

Government. Defense: aeronautics engineering and manufacturing, arms production, field medication industries, nautical manufacturing; engineering and arms research and development.

Prison: Security R&D, prison construction and design, re-education classes.

Infrastructure: Road, bridge and tunnel construction; water supply; state schools; drainage pipe construction.

Social Services: Child care, public housing construction, government-sponsored counseling, welfare.

Sin. Alcohol production and distribution, tobacco growth and processing, gambling, sex-related industries, weapons manufacture and distribution.

Transportation. Airports, buses, cabs, trains, railroad construction and ferry companies (cars cannot be included in this section due to the financing required to buy them).

*__High Tech__. Research and development of new technologies; production and manufacture of these technologies, i.e., robotics, telecommunications, space exploration, cloning, etc. (this section has an asterisk because new technologies have been known to impact society in positive and negative ways in different respects, aka disruptive technologies).

Elder Care. Assisted living facilities; geriatric nurses; retirement communities; walker, cane, personal mobility device manufacture, retail, and distribution, progressive housing (instead of modular homes, build houses easy to reform and repair for more elderly homeowners), and, finally, "Tinder for elders".

Housing. Rentals, apartment complexes, condominiums, trailers and RVs.

Higher Education. Colleges and universities (i.e., student loans, tuition, room and board fees, out-of-state fees, etc.).

Insurance. Health, car, life insurance, etc., and banking

Cosmetics. Hair care production, skin care manufacturing, makeup, designer clothes and accessories.

Maintenance. Car maintenance (i.e., mechanic, car wash, car parts and supplies, etc.), home maintenance (i.e., building materials, paint, plumbing, electric, carpentry, contracting, lawn care, landscaping, and DIY industry as a whole), storage, and the "uberization" of domestic services (in other words, personal and home care on demand).

Automation. Robotics manufacture and programming, computer manufacture and programming.

It's hard to say if anyone has ever had this kind of information before. Being able to know

the sectors of the economy that will thrive in the near future is power. However, knowledge in and of itself will not yield results. Knowledge in action is true power. In the next chapter we will outline how to put this information to use.

CHAPTER 9

WHAT TO DO WITH ALL THIS INFORMATION

My intention in writing this book is to motivate you to reevaluate your:

1. Strategic plan
2. Marketing plan
3. Financial plan

Strategic Plan: the process of evaluating a desired a future and translating that vision into action.

Why they Succeed	Why They Fail
Trust	Planning for planning's sake
Alignment	Misreading the environment
Accountability	Lack of enrollment
	Delegation by abandonment

Sales used to be an exchange of knowledge; now you can just look up just about anything. The old sales are dead. Now it's an exchange of trust. Sales has ultimately morphed into enrollment. For our purpose, we use the word "enrollment" to describe the act of enrolling oneself and/or others into a cause. In order to do this, there must be a high level of trust. Any leader must be more than an empty suit with a title.

A leader must have:

1. Congruency

The requirement to behave in alignment with authentic feelings.

2. The Best Interest for All

The thing you plan to do: an aim or purpose.

3. Capability

The ability to get something done.

4. Trade Record

Evidence of past success so others can judge what a person is willing to do.

One must trust the other. They are attempting to enroll. Then, the would-be enrollee must see evidence that you have their best interests at heart.

Below is the single best exercise I have come across in my travels for establishing a high trust environment.

"Why, How, What" Exercise

But to understand how to use this exercise, we need to understand the Leadership Ladder:

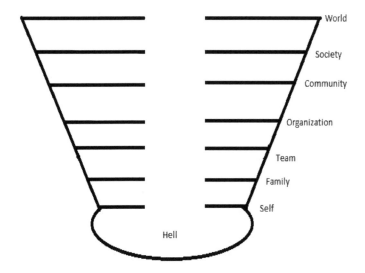

To understand the Leadership Ladder, one must recognize where one is "operating" on a regular basis, in other words, "What is my paradigm at the moment?"

I find examples are the best way to understand this: After I graduated from college, I took a position at Merrill Lynch stockbrokerage, which afforded me the ability to move out of my parents' house. I had my own apartment in New York City and was able to afford my own car and food. I was finally self-sufficient, could take care of myself, and was secure in my individual status. (I would argue that on this chart, the majority of all people are currently operating at the self level).

I experienced a paradigm shift with the birth of my first son— my reality shifted dramatically now that there was a person I would step in front of a moving bullet for. My second impulse was I needed to raise my game in my career. Having a financial mind, I did the math on all the bills that I would need to pay for the next 20 years for my son Max. This new motivation tripled the production of my business.

I was now on the family level of the leadership ladder. I would argue a successful marriage requires each partner to operate at this level. Overall statistics on the failure of marriage suggest that most partners are operating as individuals (The self level) inside a marriage.

As my practice grew, I needed to form a team of professionals to handle all the clients' needs. I needed to raise my game again in order to be at least at the team level, and in order to run multiple teams, I needed to be at the organization level. As a Vistage chair, I had to do this all over again and get to the community level.

I asked the men and women that I now led as a Vistage chair why they followed my lead, especially given that all were older than I and showcased much better business accomplishments. The unanimous answer was that I had their best interests at heart. I was there to increase the durability and sustainability of each of their companies, which was in each of their best interests. My next stage of development took my show on the road, and I now actively speak to thousands of CEOs and C-level executives each year, and arm them with knowledge to ensure the durability and sustainability of their companies in order to positively affect the North American economies (The Society Level).

Each of these intervals required my team to enable me to accomplish this new feat by taking ownership of the responsibilities that were originally mine, in order to free up my time so I could speak and inspire others. In order to do so, the team needed to be galvanized behind a cause, so that we all could leave this world a better place. That is where the "Why,

How, What" exercise comes in: to enable me, as the leader of this team, to provide Constant and Never-ending Reassurance, or C.A.N.E.R. (see Introduction).

WHY, HOW, WHAT

The next part of the exercise breaks down why and how you're doing it, and what you are doing. People doing the exercise need to make a commitment to it, and each team member needs to carry his/her own weight in order to create the results.

Most people find it easier, however, to start with what they want, and if it benefits them, then it is probably a result and belongs in the "What" category.

Each result in the "What" category needs to be S.M.A.R.T:

Specific

Measurable

Achievable

Relevant

Timely

Specific: Stresses the need for concrete criteria in order to measure progress. How will we know we've accomplished something if it is not concrete? By being specific, we can stay motivated without the vagaries that could rob us of motivation and cause doubt needlessly.

Measureable: By making the results quantifiable, we avoid ambiguity that would waste time and mental energy.

Achievable: Supporting the need to be realistic, lofty goals may sound nice, but unreachable goals may stall the team by not allowing them wins along the way.

Relevant: We need to keep our team on course by concentrating their talent and time on meaningful goals.

Timely: Refers to the need for a team to achieve milestones, to know that they are winning and as a reason for leaders to know that they're accountable.

Once a team has set all its results and is armed with their **What** questions, they will instantly know **How** they mean to operate in order to achieve their goals.

The best way I can teach **How** is to show mine. I ran an exercise with my team in order to unite them under a common purpose. What we came up with was this: "Through extensive planning and the work we do with CEOs, we firewall hundreds of companies and thousands of people so that the economy is better off for all of us having existed." When I surveyed my team, they reported to be an 11 on a scale of 1-10 in terms of how well they were doing and how good they felt.

The **How** portion of the exercise always starts with a "through" or a "by." My advice is to use the word "we" a lot, as it signifies that the team is working together. The statement must include a "so that". This way the team will understand that their work is for a higher purpose and that it will have a positive impact on society.

For example, "**Through** the economic education of others and volunteer work we firewall hundreds of companies and thousands of employees **So that** the economy is better for all of us having existed."

Lastly, but most importantly, is **Why** we all are doing this. My **Why** is to "help the few protect the many." As soon as I discovered what I now refer to as my higher purpose, my life started to dramatically change for the better. Ten years ago was the last time I had trouble getting out of bed in the morning, and I cannot count how many times I've been sick, which is powerful, considering I suffer from migraines due to a head wound I suffered when I was a child. Little, if anything, can slow me from bringing my purpose to fruition.

A **Why** statement needs to be as few words as possible—think Haiku.

Why statement needs to be:

As few words as possible and no more than six total

Powerful

Motivating

Affect as many people as possible

Think about the leadership ladder and how it positively affects a populace.

REEVALUATE YOUR MARKETING PLAN

A marketing plan usually includes information on a product or service, pricing, target market, budget, and promotion mix.

The information contained in chapters 3, 5, 6, 8 are good places to start your market research. These provide a great, 30,000-feet view from above of every country and industry that will thrive in the next decade. The way you should use this information is divided into two categories:

B to C

B to B

B to C refers to Business to Customer. In Chapter 8, we discussed all of the industries that will survive and/or thrive during a recession and are resistant to the aging of the population. If your business is on this list, you need not read this section of this chapter, just keep doing what you're doing and turn the page to the next section. But if you're not on this list, then you must develop a plan to offer new products or services that will put you on this list.

B to B means Business to Business. The list of industries that will thrive in the next decade will come in handy, and if you are on that list, you will only need to know where to diversify your windfalls. But if you're not on this list, you will need to develop a marketing strategy to attract clients who are on this list. You must also understand the businesses that you're selling to. As one Vistage member put it, "So, let me get this straight. If I am B to B, I need to know my B's C's."

For those of you considering a franchise, Chapter 8 is essential. We have already done most of the market research for you. A great example of knowing your customer is a premier guitar company we consulted with to help the company perform a series of pivots in anticipation of a decrease in their key demographic: 48-year-old white American males. This people in this demographic were declining in numbers as America started shifting from the baby boomers to gen X, starting in 2010 and lasting for approximately 14 years.

The CEO of the guitar company impressed me from the start by knowing the statistics for its industry. Most CEOs know little to nothing about demography or even who their customer really is.

The CEO described to me the three major ways this company was to pivot in the direction of a more favorable and larger demographic:

The company, under the CEO's direction, opened a guitar manufacturing plant in Mexico to create a product line of cheaper, starter guitars meant for 18-year-olds. This was much like what Harley Davidson did with the Sportster, an entry-level motorcycle that was meant for a much younger demographic than the Road King. Both of these pivots allowed for a much larger diversification of the two companies' target markets and moved the needle of its customer demographics toward a larger, younger market, while creating an aspirational business model.

The company then reintroduced the ukulele into the product line, which opened up the Asian market that was willing to pay a premium for the company's ukuleles. Not only is the ukulele popular in Asia, it is the number-one selling instrument in the world. This new product would create a new market for the company to fall back on if the guitar player demographic were to grind to a halt.

Probably the cleverest thing the CEO did was to embrace technology, as his acoustic guitars (flagship product) would not be recognized by the younger generations as the pinnacle of music technology. He began to produce YouTube videos of luthiers (guitar craftsmen) describing in detail how they make the guitars while they are making them. This demonstrated to the millennials the true quality and craftsmanship that goes into the guitars.

I offer these examples to encourage you to reposition your marketing plan in the best possible way for the next decade. Pretend your company head of sales needs to look at your company the way an investor would. For him or her to spend the limited resources of time and money wisely, using Chapter 8 is a start. If you are lucky enough to have your industry studied by the government, you need to remember that it does so passively, so this book is only a start. Your next step is to research your industry through your trade association.

Another takeaway from this story: try to work with other businesses that have the same target market and are not in competition with you or your business, just as the guitar company did with Harley Davidson. The two companies exchanged idea and strategies in order for each to better itself?

REEVALUATE YOUR INVESTMENT PLAN

Investment plan: a comprehensive assessment of an investment, current and future assets, and the objectives of these investments.

There are two major ways to look at the information given to you so far. The first is as a business owner (highly concentrated assets) and the second is as an investor. In certain cases, you can look at the information through the lens of both investor and business owner. This section is for the investor in all of us.

The lynchpin philosophy is **the stock market is not there to make you rich, it's there to keep you wealthy.** And the best strategy to staying wealthy is through diversification. I would suggest you utilize the information in Chapters 3, 5, 6, 7, and 8 to diversify investments and choose the right vehicles to invest in, knowing which countries are likely to remain stable, while producing higher returns and knowing which industries are likely to thrive.

The top ten economically stable and strong countries for the next decade:

1. Mexico
2. Brazil
3. India
4. Australia
5. Canada
6. Turkey
7. South Africa
8. New Zealand
9. Israel
10. Haiti

Top ten industries likely to survive and thrive in the next decade:

1. Maintenance
2. Agriculture
3. Elder Care
4. Death
5. Healthcare
6. Government Work
7. Insurance
8. Sin
9. Religion
10. Transportation

Tax status vulnerability of investment vehicles:

Roth IRA	
Pros	Cons
Free of any tax penalties	Tax bracket could change
Many different investment possibilities	Income limitations
No age limit	Contribution limits
Inexpensive	The government can change the tax status after the fact
Municipal Bonds	
Pros	Cons
Free of Tax Penalties	Less likely to beat inflation
Likely not as risky as the stock market	Risk of income rates changing
Very high liquidity	Risk of default*
Due to tax benefits it will compound	Not profitable for people in a low tax bracket

*Barring a reconstruction of Medicaid as a serious threat

Life Insurance (as an investment) AKA Roth IRA Alternative	
Pros	Cons
Potential returns	Mediocre Returns
Fixed Expenses	Large Expenses
Able to be withdrawn from before death	Very complicated and difficult to understand
Potential tax free income as loans	
Most voters own Life Insurance, which minimizes susceptibility to political threats	

Once again, keep in mind none of this guarantees the results that you're looking for, but ultimately this information, plus your own research, will significantly increase the likelihood of positive results.

• • •

One last story before we end. Nothing irritates me more than a C-level executive asking, at the end of my presentation, "What do you think I should do?"

I am not the expert in your field, YOU ARE!

What do I think you should do? I think you should take ownership of this challenge, do the research, and produce a better strategic, marketing, and investment plan so that the hundreds of people that you are responsible for can continue to feed their families with a stable income, without having to worry about a sudden market collapse or decrease in the number of people in the target market because you read this book and prepared for all of that.

Do whatever it takes to produce Constant And Never Ending Reassurance (C.A.N.E.R) to show that your employees and yourself, for that matter, will have a steady income in 5 years.

You will be able to sleep soundly, and so will all your employees, customers, and loved ones. Everyone will be happier as a result of you reading this book without even knowing that you read it.

Good luck and happy hunting!

33556535R00113

Made in the USA
Middletown, DE
15 January 2019